T0146937

How GOD SHOWS Up

A Compelling Story Following the Sudden Death of a
Child and a Mother's Determination to Find and Know
Her Daughter's Eternal Expression of Life

JUDITH MARIE RN, MA, MSW

BALBOA.
PRESS
A DIVISION OF HAY HOUSE

Balboa Press books may be ordered through booksellers or by contacting:

Balboa Press
A Division of Hay House
1663 Liberty Drive
Bloomington, IN 47403
www.balboapress.com
1 (877) 407-4847

Because of the dynamic nature of the Internet, any web addresses or links contained in this book may have changed since publication and may no longer be valid. The views expressed in this work are solely those of the author and do not necessarily reflect the views of the publisher, and the publisher hereby disclaims any responsibility for them.

The author of this book does not dispense medical advice or prescribe the use of any technique as a form of treatment for physical, emotional, or medical problems without the advice of a physician, either directly or indirectly. The intent of the author is only to offer information of a general nature to help you in your quest for emotional and spiritual well-being. In the event you use any of the information in this book for yourself, which is your constitutional right, the author and the publisher assume no responsibility for your actions.

Scriptures taken from the Holy Bible, New International Version®, NIV®. Copyright © 1973, 1978, 1984, 2011 by Biblica, Inc.™ Used by permission of Zondervan. All rights reserved worldwide. www.zondervan.com The "NIV" and "New International Version" are trademarks registered in the United States Patent and Trademark Office by Biblica, Inc.™

Any people depicted in stock imagery provided by Thinkstock are models, and such images are being used for illustrative purposes only. Certain stock imagery © Thinkstock.

Print information available on the last page.

ISBN: 978-1-5043-8749-1 (sc)
ISBN: 978-1-5043-8751-4 (hc)
ISBN: 978-1-5043-8750-7 (e)

Library of Congress Control Number: 2017914076

Balboa Press rev. date: 11/14/2017

"Through suffering the sudden devastating death of her beloved young daughter and the poignancy of the deep grief and lingering sadness that paralyzed her, Judith Marie shares her amazing story of healing. She also reveals the blessing of grace that came in the form of a joyous and loving marriage with deep spiritual connection. She takes readers on an inspiring journey of discovering the eternal existence of living love. Her experience moving through the process of grieving and finding love and joy once again is an inspiration to anyone who has experienced the loss of a child or loved one. This is a must-read for all seekers of the Spiritual Wisdom inherent within us and how God shows up for us all."

—Drs. H. Ronald and Mary Hulnick, Co-Directors, University of Santa Monica

CONTENTS

Part 3 – Living with Emily

Part 4 – Life with James Thornton Daily

Part 5 – Personal History

DEDICATION

First, I want to dedicate this book to my daughter, Emily Janel who lives in Heaven. She will forever be my teacher to a greater presence of God with me. And second, to my former husband Jim for bringing the loving presence of God into our relationship in ways beyond measure.

Furthermore, I give my full heart of gratitude to John-Roger for being the marvelous way shower of loving always longed for. Years ago, after accepting the Christ relationship through Jesus, I asked, "Now, after accepting, how do I walk it in my life?" John-Roger—and now John Morton, the current Spiritual Director of the Movement of Spiritual Inner Awareness (MSIA)—have been the greatest of beings for the teachings and blessings of that awakening and guidance. As I have asked, the teachers appear in many ways and experiences through this divinely led movement of my spiritual inner awareness with all those who have joined with me along the way.

I close with the Hebrew words *Baruch bashan* (bay-roosh bay-shan), meaning "as I ask, the blessings already are."

ACKNOWLEDGMENTS

First, I want to thank my wonderful family: Mom and Dad, who will always reside within me. Then, my brother, Ted, my sisters, Pamela and Beth, and their wonderful spouses and children, who have followed with caring hearts and ever-present hugs. Their healing sustenance through all of my tears, grief, and growth held me together in this lifetime. I send y'all heartfelt hugs and kisses from wherever I am, morning, noon, or night, as I lift you into God's loving in all ways that can be delivered.

Then, my gratitude goes beyond measure for the opportunity that has been given to me with the Women Writing in Birmingham class created and facilitated by Lucy Jaffe in the setting of her lovely home on the cliff overlooking Birmingham, Alabama. In addition to her guidance and participation, my great privilege and joy has been to meet and receive the support of all the women participants over nine years of semesters. We have gathered to pursue our many voices and stories, which we freely express in a safe, confidential place where we write, read, listen, and give feedback for encouragement and support. Without this milieu I would not have found the courage that my heart has held and the joy that I have come to know from the life returned to me that I share in these pages. Thank you, Lucy, and all the women who have held me up and listened through my tears, my joy, and all my fumbling toward clarity with my words. Your words of encouragement and your presence of support have kept me persevering to completion!

PREFACE

My Purpose and Process for Writing

My purpose for my current writing is threefold. First, I want to share the journey of my healing—that is, my letting go of my most precious gift and finding trust and renewal in God. I want to share how my relationship with God became a reality of knowing the eternal life of my daughter after her passing, beyond an imposed belief that I would need to *wait to see her again after I too passed over.* This waiting that I was expected to trust and accept felt shallow and without consideration or evidence of what I had heard was the eternal life where she now resided. *If life is eternal, then I wanted to find that place that went on living with her, and I wanted to find it NOW!* I did not intend to *wait for someday* I could not survive without knowing more about what was available and true through the faith I had always had in my relationship with God. I want to share how that loving presence has *shown up* for me.

Secondly, in writing, I aim to step through the massive fear and darkness of loss to share what I learned about connecting this lifetime to her eternal source of life. I want to share with you how I came to know the depth of that source of life, to find and go forward with the abundance of it, as I had joyfully experienced in the gift of her physical presence; to share how God and I co-created experiences and interactions with her existence from the other side. I want to share how her eternal presence became a reality as I grew in greater awareness of Christ within me.

Thirdly, I want to share some feedback that was initiated when my mother lovingly let me know that she had learned that the loss of a child was something I would "get over". She let me know she had attended a professional presentation after worrying about my grieving. Now, after reading some current research, I see the kind of findings she referred to. Research shows significant elevated mortality rates in women and mothers who grieve the loss of a child. The studies cover families of every social status, financial means, family size, age, marital status, and religious orientation, regardless of the course or situation of the death of the child. It confirmed my own experience and was startling to once again bring this to my attention. The time frame of these studies showed a 133 percent increase in suicide during the first two years after the loss and an increase in ongoing health issues up to 18 years, then ongoing effects throughout life. This includes a variety of ways that depression shows up and the variety of ways it can be expressed in response to the death of a child.[1]

I not only understand all the factors, but I share the awareness and experience as I write my story. Even though I was a professional with education in psychiatry and human development, I wanted to end my life. I desired to leave this life to be with my daughter and be free from the intense pain of separation. For a while, a real part of me saw it as a logical solution. I struggled to get through each day as a childless mother living alone, trying to cope without direction or purpose in my life. I also had other influences that gave me answers and reengagement of purpose.

---

[1] Rogers, Catherine H., Frank J. Floyd et al. "Long-term Effects of the Death of a Child on Parents' Adjustment in Midlife," *J. Fam. Psychol.* 2008 Apr 22(2): 203–211.

MY INITIAL PROCESS
WITH POETRY

What Am I Waiting For?

I hear others saying this to me without speaking,
or perhaps it is that voice from within that
projects this reflection from experiences long past.
I am obsessed at times with impatience and
with incompletions that sit in front of me
calling for my attention to get them "out of the way."
I say that I am waiting for "things" to get done
so then ... I can have some creative time for me.
You know the agenda:
All the home care, self-care, management issues,
but as I write, I am more honest with myself,
wondering what really blocks my expression – takes me off course?
I need time to be quiet without distractions,
I need to be quiet with myself,
disallowing all of the distractions around and within me.
I want less to be done: less that needs to be done.
But then there *needs* to be time enough, and the right moments.
I want permission to just stay on course
with the direction in my mind's eye.
Permission, support, and encouragement to write ...

Inspiration and self-approval …
I hear, *I already have what I need.*
My own creativity is ready to accompany me.
She's shown her presence with such an elegance of beauty.
We've had a few dances, and the music is waiting.
So what is at the heart of this waiting?
Waiting to find the course of my writing?
As I quiet myself and listen, I hear …
for Emily to come home.
Loudly and clearly I hear, *I'm waiting for Emily to come home.*
In my heart there will always be a space that waits for her,
Through all of the healing and knowing, there is still a space in
    waiting.
A space that thinks something isn't completed:
one more thing to do … *one more*
accomplishment for learning and letting go,
one more place to love;
Out there, in here, for others, for myself, and for the world.
Passing time, I wait, without *really* knowing what stops me.
Creating means new life. Emily was already my perfect creation.
I keep doing—waiting for her to show up.
If I'm pleasing to others, pleasing to God, pleasing to me—*Please, God!*

Listening, I hear and am reminded
God will give her a key so she can drop by to see me.
It has happened frequently from the other side.
I move into sleep and travel into my Soul Self, and our Selves
    could meet
Without the restrictions of this body.
I've heard others speak of it.
This body *here* is too busy—a "busy body" is what I am.
I've heard this phrase before, "busy body," without much
    attention to it.
But now I know what it is… my busy body:

It feels best to pass through time quickly by keeping busy
Doing … I've done it since Emi left.

There must be something more to do. There always is.
I never have to look very far. It greets me:
clearing, cleansing, caring, reaching out, touching, smiling, speaking;
finding more connections of things to do.
It's like a deep riveted vibration in my body:
this doing, wanting to find my being … of myself, as me,
     without her.
Fearing that I did not do something I should have done.
Remembering her hand nestled in mine: in the car, walking along,
chatting of the day, negotiating for what's happening next,
laughing and cheering the contents of life and loving.
I just go on, searching to know of her presence within
finding new ways to live and love again.
The journey is ongoing. I am the one who will now persevere
     to the end,
carrying with me this teacher of joy and brilliance.

Just now, she has shown up again as my teacher,
showing me how I've used her life and leaving to create,
not functionally but dysfunctionally,
a disconnect from loving and creating for myself.
I forgive myself for holding on to her
in ways that are of disservice to me.
Again, grateful for finding this new place in me
that has shown up for my loving,
I embrace this place for my Self to once again
offer a new freedom for expressing with my Soul:
the gifts of Spirit that show up for my words to be made clear.
Who is this gift of Spirit?
Do you have a name?
I listen in the Silence and my words flow.

INTRODUCTION

Something Is Lost

Someone has suddenly disappeared. The lost person is my daughter. Her body died, and I don't know where to find her. I spent years asking and searching for her, sometimes out loud, sometimes in my writing, and always within. "What happened?" I asked. "How did I let this occur to my sweet daughter? How did I miss taking care of her when she needed me?" I ask myself and my God—whoever is listening in there—"Emily, where are you?"

I heard, "God only knows," which feels like a bit of sarcasm from my childhood. I heard that phrase many times from my family as I grew up. It showed up when a question seemed unanswerable. "God only knows" was said or heard as one gave up a quest for answers.

But now I say, "Okay, God, since you are the One who knows, please show me." I say, "I need you to take me to her. I need to see her one more time." *Silence. There is only silence.* I get louder: "Where is she, God? I'm her mom! It's *my* job to take care of her. You gave me this job, and I love having it. You brought her to me, Lord, and gave me all this loving and joy with the gift and miracle of her life. What now? Now what? What is this, God? What *more* do you want from me?" I was broken and lost. I lost my favorite job: employed by God. The rug that held my feet had just been pulled out from under me. How do I stand up when I feel so taken apart? Where do I turn? How do I see and find my way? My mind and body are filled with confusion, and a physical and mental numbness renders me dysfunctional. From unspoken fears and guilt, the tears roll unceasingly! My searching began in the despairing silence of God's voice.

Yes, my story is waiting to be told. The healing and writing it down has now taken years. Many times I had started it and spoken of it, but I have come to a place now where I can embrace my experience with gratitude for my own life, which continued after the sudden death of my daughter, Emily. I can now write the story, knowing that I want to share it with the purpose of expanding my gratitude for all of the ways a Loving Spirit ultimately shows up and offers support and caring to all those who have gone or need to go through that valley of the death of a child. Death is a treacherous conviction with an irreversible ending, but I refused to accept the unviable sentence of it, particularly with regards to my beautiful and gifted daughter who brought so much joy and loving to this planet and to my life.

Besides the fact that her life was so very beautiful in many ways and I was unwilling to give it up, I had to deal with the huge gap of reality that she was no longer with me. I was raised, had studied, and chose to believe that life given by God is eternal. I needed to find out how the truth of that actually existed. I am ready to share with you the ways of that realization and how I came to find it. I have received the experience of it in many ways, which I will disclose.

Writing it down revealed places in me that had not fully accepted my loss and needed healing along the way. Writing the story was like reliving it all over again, and visions of lack and loss arose from within for me to face again. At times, I had to release pain and face loss and fear to regain stability before I could once again look at the paper.

So now, here are my writings of finding and knowing, from

my own experience, that my daughter lives as I live; though not physically in this body, she has shown up as very real and alive within me. She came as my teacher, as we all are to each other, but I knew she was a particular teacher for me when her sweet spirit came in on the day of her birth June 1, 1972. Yes, my story is waiting to be told. In fact, you are the witness of my process, and for that I am grateful. I ask for this witness from you and from all those Souls and beings from the other side of this physical life to assist me and be with me on this journey. For that I am also in deep gratitude. I am grateful for finding the presence of my Soul's journey, that I might also be more awake and fully aware of how this presence within me and within all of us is truly the place for finding this eternal life. Saying and reading the scriptures to believe is one thing, but practicing the knowing of them and the practical living of them as a life-giving agent with all of their dimensions is another.

"So how did you do it?" you ask.

Attending Women Writing Birmingham classes in Birmingham, Alabama, has given me a place to condense this practical portion of my life into an epistle on paper. It happens at the circle gathering, along with the candlelight that we pass for intention and confidentiality. It creates, for me, a safe place to find courage and the ability to express from my heart. The inspiration shows up in realizing all I need do is bring myself to look and listen and join the camaraderie within this circle of women writing it down. As I receive their feedback on this work, their encouragement has kept me going. I just keep signing up to be there.

One such morning, knowing that class was about to convene, I asked; what is the image for today, the next chapter of my life to be written? I heard these words, *How God Shows Up*, as a theme for my life. That's the way I heard it, "How God Shows Up." Well … that would be the truth! Throughout my life, there has always been an evident caring for me that has *shown up* even though it was sometimes surprising to me when it happened. I wasn't expecting that, through Emily's death, I would come to have the experience that was the setup for *my learning* in this lifetime. It was a time of feeling totally abandoned by God, separated from my own Soul and Oneness with that Great Source of Loving that I had always known. It was an illusion of separation that I had not known during all my years of studying the scriptures and loving my relationship with God. Simply put, I had never felt so ineffective and out of control. It challenged and rendered me helpless. I had no sense that there was anything greater than the sudden death of my child. In my life I had needed to find my way, with God's help and grace, through the many events of growing up, marriage, childbirth, divorce, and single parenting. This one hit me so hard that none of the rest seemed to count any longer. Not that those experiences weren't valuable for teaching that we truly have no control. It's just that this one rendered me helpless beyond all the others.

Truly, the way I have been able to acknowledge my experience, find the learning, and create meaning for it all has been to realize that there is a Higher Presence that has a greater purpose for teaching me what I am here for—that there is a greater and bigger God than I had allowed.

The suddenness and shock of this experience persuaded me that I would need to dig deeply to lift myself from the prevailing darkness of great loss, pain, separation, and helplessness. I felt a numbness that was disabling and lonesome. *Very* lonesome! My grief was beyond what others around me wanted to approach or touch. Not only did I hurt immensely, but I also felt responsible for the hurt that others around me felt. Their sympathy and pain were palpable to me as they wondered what they would do if they were in my shoes. This was not what I intended for my life. I was used to and much more comfortable with bringing joy and something of encouragement and uplift others, and this was *not* it!

So I searched to find reason and cause. I searched inwardly

with my fragile and damaged heart where I had asked God to reside through the man Jesus Christ. I was committed to find the walk that went with the talk that I heard over and over. Now was that time. I found (and find) that this earth is but one universe set up particularly for the purpose of disclosing the greater meaning of our experiences and existence. I want to share with you how I found my way through it and what my Soul's journey has been to this point in time. I found this bigger vision within the greatest gifts of my lifetime: the birth of my daughter, her sudden departure eleven years later, the grieving, and the process of finding and awakening to something greater than death.

What the experiences have been and how they showed up have amazed me, and for that I am grateful. I received this immense and lifesaving learning beginning with Emily's death in 1983. It became the eventual preparation for knowing, experiencing, and finding eternal life that together prepared me for the passing of my husband, Jim, twenty-four years later, in 2007.

I still have vivid memories of events that I can safely say are imbedded into my vision and knowing that I can recall for sharing to this day. They showed up as events that were for my healing as an expansion of awareness to something greater than I had known. They are wisdoms of comfort that I have learned to know as a truth of loving that replaces all the massive illusions of death and grieving. I asked for courage and strength, and here is how it showed up. This is my story.

PART ONE

EMILY JANEL

CHAPTER 1

Courage in the Face of Death

I can see that my life has been filled with steps of courage that built upon each other.

1. As a young person out of high school in 1962, I became the first women in our large family who went to college. My high school counselor told me I would never make it in college. I did.

2. I graduated in 1967 with an associate's degree and passed my exams to become a registered nurse. I created an income greater than my brilliant father ever received during all his years of being lost in labor work.

3. I married in 1967 and then divorced seven years later when I knew that the loving commitment had been lost.

4. I gave birth to my daughter, Emily, in 1972 successfully with natural childbirth to welcome her consciously as she arrived.

5. I parented Emily as a single mom while earning a master's degree in growth and development. Emily was the inspiration for this work.

6. I pioneered a brand-new career when I became the child life specialist at Borgess Medical Center in Kalamazoo,

Michigan, in 1980, after receiving an invitation from the pediatric staff manager and director.

7. All were preparation for the greatest task of courage: the sudden death of Emily at eleven years of age on August 11, 1983. Little did I know that her passing was going to be part of the life agenda that I was to fulfill.

My job as a child life specialist was to support children and their parents during hospital admission. We offered play therapy, school support, and education for the developmental and psychosocial needs of the children and their families during hospitalization. I was available to assist others with their losses and challenges with their children, but I had not considered that I also would awaken to my own trauma and pain. I look back at the depth of my grief and how my healing took place. "What happened?" you ask. Thank you for asking. Thank you also for listening. It helps me to talk about it. It helps me to write and then read it aloud. It's as if the more witnesses I gathered, the more I was lifted above the shocking truth of it.

I was working in the pediatric unit on the sixth floor at Borgess Medical Center when the phone call arrived. It wasn't long after 3:00 p.m. on August 11, 1983.

I picked up the phone as I entered my office and sat down with weakened knees as I heard on the line, "Mrs. Losey, this is the emergency room doctor in Three Rivers, Michigan. Your daughter Emily is here with us. She was brought in by ambulance following a 911 call from Camp Wakeshma that she had fallen over during play and was not breathing. All possible efforts for resuscitation have been made, and we are continuing our efforts for you to come and be here with her."

"What are you saying?" I heard myself call out into the phone. I ran out into the hallway and to the front desk looking for a doctor. "Please pick up line three and tell me what they are saying. A doctor from an emergency room is calling about Emily." I blurted this out to one of the pediatricians who stood nearby. She picked up the line and listened as I paced nearby. She then reached her arm around me. Other nurses and staff had gathered around as they heard my call for help. Maggie, a nurse and friend, had already gotten my purse and told me she would take me to Emily. The facility was about thirty minutes away. Inwardly I began to call out to God.

I had just run back from assisting a mom whose child had coded in the pediatric clinic on the ground floor. It was one of our children with cystic fibrosis that I knew well, with a mom who I expected might be alone. Christopher had quit breathing, resuscitation had been administered, and he had recovered.

The call related that Emily was being resuscitated, but she was not responding. At the same time this child with cystic fibrosis was coding, my daughter had suddenly fallen over as she went to kick the soccer ball at camp. She had wanted to spend time at this camp to be with some of her friends from school who had attended in prior years. She was the star goalie for her local team and wanted to go to camp this year for the first time to enjoy the experiences she heard in stories from her friends.

The soccer-camp staff had begun CPR within a minute of her falling. They quickly called 911 for help. Once they had her in the emergency room, they searched to find me. My mind went numb as I heard what I thought they were saying. I couldn't repeat it or say the words.

My mind was racing with disbelief. I was at work helping children who were hospitalized and in need of thoughtful attention. Who was with my daughter and listening to her need for help? What happened? Who could tell me? I prayed on the way, "Please, Lord God, you know how much I love the children. Please, please don't make me go through this!" But Emily and God had something else going. My motherhood that I cherished so much and my love for children would not be bargained for with God.

3

I walked into the ER where Emily lay, her body warm with the loving service of this team of people. I ran to her to let her know I was there. "I'm here, Emily! Mommy's here with you! Emily, Emily, Mommy's here with you!" I kissed and hugged her as I looked for her response. I begged inwardly to have her return to this beautiful eleven-year-old growing body. My thoughts and prayers swirled with the longing for God to bring her back and let her reawaken and join us. *Now, God, please bring her back as only You can, God. Please bring her back.* I called out from within … but it was not to be. Not this time. My heart sank with the pain of her lifeless presence.

What had happened? What could possibly have happened that I was not informed of so I could help her? *How did this come to happen, Lord?* The unbearable guilt and pain began to set in that somehow I had made a mistake, not attending to her needs. How was I to go on living without her?

The attending staff and doctor continued trying to resuscitate her, pressing air into her lungs with an Ambu bag and compressing her chest for circulation of blood and allowing me my tears of realization. They asked if I would like to hold her. "Yes, yes, please let me hold her," I cried. They lifted her, encased by the white sheeting holding her long browned legs and 5'1" body, and I cuddled her for the last time. Tears rolled down my cheeks and onto hers as I took in the fragrance of her and kissed her face and told her how much I loved her. I thanked her for coming to be my precious child and waited for her joyful response.

Time was passing, and they asked if I would like to donate her organs for assisting another child. "Yes," I whispered as I looked into their eyes for strength. I know now that I was shifting from mommy to pediatric nurse. I recognized what they were asking and realized that I knew the questions and what they were about. I knew children who needed this support. It was more than I knew I could give. It would be a last gift of her body to give life to another. It was now an option to share a part of her to have life renewed for someone else when hers was not viable.

I returned her to the team for further work to maintain the oxygenation and circulation of blood through her body. A staff person arrived with the forms on a clipboard. I struggled through my tears to see what I was signing, and with shaky hands I scrawled my name on the papers. Emily was then wheeled out of the ER on the gurney where she had spent the last few hours and was taken to a surgical suite. I was later told that she would be donating her corneas and kidneys and another organ that I don't clearly recall.

I then sat down in a nearby private room to call her dad, who was in a city further away. He had been with her for a week, ending two days before she left for camp. He arrived in time to see her body and say good-bye after the procedures. We agreed to give permission for an autopsy, and the two of us signed more papers. I was told that a full autopsy would be conducted. The ER doctor was also the local medical examiner for the county. He told me he would be available to me as often as I needed.

Numbness set in to my mind and body. It was a shock that took time from me. My mind swirled and my heart ached with the thought of walking away without her. The finality of her life left me without words. It was a moment in time of deadening silence.

Family members had been notified and my mother and my sister Pam arrived at the ER as well as a couple of parents of Emily's friends who were at camp with her. They left to get back to the camp to see how their children were being attended to. Mom was still recovering from Dad's passing three years earlier, and she walked in without emotion at the possible reality of what was happening. She refused to join me in my tears. I remember her driving me home, with my tears flowing; I thought they would never cease.

How could I go home and be there without Emily? Mom

dropped me off and departed to be with my fourteen-year-old sister Beth, who didn't yet know the outcome. I went into our home on Timber Oaks Drive in Plainwell, Michigan, and as I moved down the hall to face Emily's bedroom and mine, I began to call out to God. I entered her room with the pink checked spread on her bed with its white antiqued headboard and curved footboard. Her small desk was covered with her writing and coloring utensils. She had placed pictures of her favorite animals on the wall, and she had specially chosen the rainbow decal on the window.

I cried out to God to tell me why. What was I to learn from this? What was the good that would come from this? How would I go on living with this heavy heart of *death*? Where now was this *eternal life* that I knew of and read of and confessed in the Apostles Creed every Sunday in church? If Emily was in heaven as I believed, then I wanted to know where that was and go there to be with her. God had given her to me to take care of her. My job wasn't finished, and I wanted to continue on with the miraculous gift of her life. In tears, I fell onto the brown shag rug. Penny, Emily's cocker spaniel, was cuddled nearby with a sock in her mouth, wanting to know where Emily was. Her wagging tail told me she was sure Emily would come home as always.

The shock of this event felt confusing and disorderly to me. Someone, somewhere in this scenario, must have made a mistake. It was all wrong inside me. My pain could not have come from a loving God, as I knew it, and I would take care of her as was ordained with her birth from my womb. No one had told me what to do or be in a circumstance like this, and I would seek out and find the error of this situation. I would search and know what to do next. I wouldn't allow her to be taken from me. God and I knew better. I was sure of it! I would seek and find His assistance for knowing to understand what this was.

A Poem for Courage

"Courage" is the momentum of my writing life.

It whispers in my ear as my heart speaks the words I put on paper:

Episodes of stories that radiate with loving, devotion, and healing

from the grief and challenges gone by,

the episodes of my life when I stepped forward with renewed
courage,

time when my heart felt its greatest pain of loss and abandonment.

From somewhere the strength to go on.

My heart knows of courage even though my body and mind

will oftentimes pull me into *discouragement.*

A process of stepping forward and standing up one more time
than I've fallen

into an abyss of numbness, shock, and escape—

a depth from a source of *encouragement* that lifts me.

What a great word from my *discouraging* illusions

to *encouragement* and all the resources that come to me for
deliverance.

And where are these places of *encouragement?* How do they look?

What makes them work?

A person to offer a loving touch or words of support.

A smile of a stranger that greets me with silent eyes of caring.

A safe place that allows my voice to be heard.

A teacher who simply says to put the seat of my pants on the seat
of a chair with a piece of paper and pen so I can "let go and
let God."

Listening for words that appear as witness of companionship from
an inner source.

The still small voice that speaks, "I Am with you all ways."

I ask, I listen, I hear, I write and then read for my awareness.

Courage shows up—a deep place in my heart that kindles the
flame

Of life that moves on.

CHAPTER 2

The Funeral

Family and friends gathered at the funeral home a block off the main street in our small town of Plainwell. Neighborhood homes were adjacent to this small but lovely and comfortable facility. It was a single-level light brown brick building that sat on the corner with a wide double front door to one side. Visitation was for two days prior to the funeral service, and families and children came by to visit with me, offer their respects, and speak of their love for Emily.

All white casket and contributions at Funeral

One fifth-grader who lived in the neighborhood came in quietly by herself. Finding Emily there in the casket, she quickly exited before I could speak to her. Soon she came in again with her mother. As I approached them to see who they were, she told me her name and introduced her mom. She spoke with some speech difficulty and added, "Emily was always nice to me." It touched me deeply to hear this child speak with such tender gratitude for Emily, to hear of her kindness to others, no matter their abilities. I thanked her for sharing with me. It was a precious moment.

Children were invited to bring something to put in the casket with her. Stickers were a popular choice. My niece Stephanie told me that she has a memory of seeing rainbow stickers in the casket. The current collection trend was stickers of all sorts. Emily had a large collection neatly categorized in a decorated three-ring notebook. She also loved and read all the Garfield cartoons at the time, and Stephanie recalls a stuffed Garfield being in the casket with her.

The service was given by the two pastors from Twin Lakes Reformed Church. Pastor Verlyn Hemmen and Pastor Dave Schreuder told me that they had agreed to write a service for Emily and then see who would present. They saw that they would *both* share from their ministry and their two very different experiences in knowing Emily and our family. I do not recall the content although they did pass on their copies to me afterward, but I am aware that it was comforting, and I felt the presence of God attending there with us.

One of the pastors had been chaplain for the week at our church camp on Lake Michigan with Emily and others from church. I was grateful to hear stories and learn of her experiences of joy and friendship that had occurred when I was not with her. I wanted people to talk about her and how they enjoyed being with her. It was comforting to hear how others knew her. I was not connected to the reality of her absence and felt fearful. I found myself questioning whether she had really been here. It validated her actual presence when others shared stories of being with her.

The next part of the funeral was more difficult for me. I blocked this incident from my memory and now, thirty-one years later, I am recalling the scene. After the funeral service, I watched people exit to the sidewalk outside and wait for the casket to be carried out. As I looked out, I saw that one person waiting outside was actually smiling even laughing some. I was aghast and offended that someone could smile and laugh at such a time! I couldn't imagine ever being able to smile again. I was amazed and felt a depth of sorrow and loss when I saw it.

I was then escorted out a side door and seated in the limousine that would follow the hearse bringing the casket and Emily to the cemetery. We sat there for what seemed a long time, and I was ready to bolt from this foreign vehicle and see what was happening. My friend Gayle, who sat with me, comforted me and kept me calm, and finally we departed. We were on our way to the consecration of Emily's body to the ground. At that time in 1983, it was customary for family and friends to follow the hearse in parade formation with designated flags on their cars as part of a funeral procession.

We arrived at the country cemetery where our family had four plots. It sat between a field of cattle and the caretaker's house and was bordered by the freeway in the distance and the small country road where we entered. We pulled onto a grassy two-lane drive up next to the plot where my dad had been buried three years earlier. Emily would be buried next to Papa. The grave was already dug, and the platform was ready, with a green grass cover to receive the casket. Family members and Mr. Vermeulen, Emily's favorite teacher, carried the closed white casket to the platform.

As everyone parked in and around the cemetery, we were led to gather around the site. On the side where the hole was dug, there were six or eight chairs for family members. I was led to a seat in the center of the chairs. As I approached, I invited others—Emily's father and family and my family—to sit with me. My dear friend Gayle, who'd flown in from Oregon, was nearby. (Gayle was like a second mom to Emily for the years we went to college classes in California. She cared for Emily and I for her son Jeremy on a weekly basis for several semesters. I was grateful to have her with me.)

As I sat surrounded by empty chairs, no one else came to sit with me. I invited others again to sit, but no one responded. No one was moving in my direction. My family, Emily's father, Chuck, and his family, were all there, but no one looked at me or made a move toward the chairs. The pastor stood across from me on the other side of the hole, next to Emily in the casket, and I was there with my feet close by the edge of the hole with a row of chairs where no one wanted to sit.

I spoke again. "Will someone please sit with me?" The silence and abandonment that I felt as I faced this ordeal was devastating. I looked up and saw others watching me. I could see Emi in my mind's eye inside the casket wearing the new shorts I had promised her when she got home from camp, a favorite purple top, and the golden butterfly necklace that I bought for both of us to wear together forever. And now here I was with my feet braced next to the long deep hole in the ground with empty chairs on either side.

The pastor began to share our purpose for being here, but I couldn't listen to him. I stood up with the big empty dark hole in front of me, "I can't sit here by myself!" I said. Then I bolted. The anxiety, discomfort, and abandonment were unbearable! I picked my way through the crowd and headed down the grassy path out of the cemetery, marched onto the street, and set out for home. I was not going to sit there by myself, as if accepting something I was sure should not have happened, and put my daughter into the ground!

I was charging down the road when Gayle caught up with

me. Everyone else stayed in their proper places around the grave, while I was becoming a person I'd never been before! I wasn't going to do it! Gayle stopped my getaway, held on to me, and led me back. We stood in the rear as the service continued. I was the first to get back into the limo to return to the church where a reception was to be held. I didn't bother to invite anyone to come along. No one spoke to me nor I to them that I can recall. The sense of abandonment was piercing. I wanted them all to move to their cars so we could move out ASAP. I sat in tears in the big black car and waited. I really don't remember anything after that for the next couple of weeks.

CHAPTER 3

Warm-Ups for Writing It Down

EMILY JANEL

Not to Be Forgotten—Notes to Self from 1983

She had spent a week on vacation with her father.

We had less than twenty-four hours together before it was time to be on our way.

Time to get ready for Camp Wakeshma for soccer with friends.

She talked unendingly, filling the time with all that she had done

while getting ready—and not getting ready for:

What she needed to bring

What she needed to wear

Reading her last *Bananas* magazine

Telling me all of the jokes

"Help me get ready, Mom!"

Talking to her "huppy" dog: "Don't have your puppies before I return."

We sat together and read a catalog while the dryer finished.

"Please help me around the house, Emi. You and I are partners again."

Dave won't be coming back. I'm surprised, but I feel okay about it.

You and I did a good job of learning how to be a step-family.

It's not your fault that Dave left.

We'll try to move into the house next door—

To stay here in the neighborhood, at your school as I promised.

I've seen it. I think you'll like it!

We have an appointment to see it—when you return from camp.

I'm working on a money-making project. Come help me?" I asked.

"We need to go now, have to stop at my office and pick up your health forms.

I didn't get your physical forms filled out—

Oh well, it is not needed.

I'm so glad we did it though ….

It was such a nice experience together.

You've shared more with me since then.

How your body has grown!

You're becoming so beautifully developed.

Thank you for talking to me about your menses this month.

I'm glad it came before vacation and camp, too.

While we're here at the hospital,

Let's stop and see Uncle Estes on the third floor.

They will love seeing how much you've grown.

You are so special to me."

I loved walking arm-in-arm with you down the hallway that Sunday afternoon.

"What? You forgot your shin-guards?

Well, okay, one more stop before we get to camp.

I love you so much, Emily.

I'm sorry I got irritated with you earlier …

When you shuffled around … not getting ready and packed up.

Let's take every last minute until you have to be there to check in

Just being together."

Thank You, God, for bringing us together again that day.

Two days prior to Emily's death she awoke very ill.

She told Rachel, her friend next to her,

"My head hurts so much that I can't move it on my pillow."

She complained of dizziness but was without a stomachache or fever.

She vomited in the breakfast line, and Kathy took her to the health officer.

He gave her one Tylenol and sent her on her way.

She rested and wanted to play.

Five times, the log states, Emily returned for help with her headache that continued. (Angie says six, because she went with her the night before the log states, when the headache began.) The coaches kept telling her she could sit out and watch. She did that too. Her teammates say she was grabbing her head and her stomach that morning as she tried to play. Natalie saw her on the ground and came to help her up, after most of the others were gone.

"I blacked out for a few seconds," said Emi, "but don't tell anyone. You know, my dad nearly died once. I died once too when I was in the hospital for scarlet fever. Papa died, and we buried him."

Her friends wondered, *Emi, why are you talking about dying?* "You'll die, and we'll bury you in your soccer clothes," they answered jokingly.

They rested extra long that day. A tour group visited and needed escort. Emi went for another Tylenol. The regular health officer had a day off. Someone else gave her an Extra-Strength Tylenol from her purse. Amy said she looked pale with bags under her eyes just before they went back out for another game of soccer.

Her coach told us, "Emi said she was ready for a great game!"

The warm-up exercises had started.

The ball ricocheted and came toward Emi.

She went for the ball and fell forward to the ground.

She faced Ginger on the ground with her face red and sweaty, gasping for breath.

"C'mon, Em! Get up," said Anna, who thought she must be joking.

Her body began to jerk, and her nearby coach yelled for help.

Her son began CPR, and someone ran for the van.

The ER staff received her exactly as I saw her two hours later when I arrived.

Inspiration from Gratitude

My calling to write comes from an Inspiration of Gratitude
To be of service onto the pages.
Here I am showing up again for the now renewed calling to write.
What does this calling of my writing have to say to me?
What is this momentum of service to myself and others who meet
    this valley of grief?
The vision I get is that I am approaching the precipice of a grand
    canyon.
I am about to fly off into the vastness of it.
It is full of excitement and anticipation but also fear and trepidation!
Am I equipped for flight? We'll see.
I sense myself holding on and holding back.
I need a new definition of putting myself on the edge at the verge
    of flying
Out over the canyon—as beautiful as it is.
A flight that comes as a calling, an invitation from wings soaring,
sharing the beauty, the joy, the fears, the grief and
    the process for passing through it to life unending.
The process is in all the ways that courage has shown up
    and led me to the awareness of the strength of my heart.
My heart holds the shimmers of Light that inspire through
    gratitude: my wings for flight!
It is new to me to have this awareness of writing from a place of
    gratitude;
not that I haven't known of it, but that I haven't used it as such.
Even now as I say it and write, I know that owning gratitude is
    my tool for writing.
It is new and fresh: has a simple "feels *good*" about it.
I set aside my former thoughts: an imagined need for a huge mind-
    full of memories and chatter that covers my life experience
    of what might be meaningful to write about, including
    judgments that appear overwhelming and inadequate.

17

Constantly thinking about it was simply scary and filled with fears of failure, lack, and loss. Resistance appeared as forgetfulness looking for blame, hurt, and loss. A forgetfulness that disembodies my knowing and gets me *no*-where!

However, coming from Gratitude and Thankfulness gives me a renewed flow.

Expressing more clearly from my heart has given me this inspiration from the beginning

When I became aware that I could find my way through my loss and pain of grieving.

The discovery of writing from gratitude is a self-loving momentum for writing my story.

I'm ready for the next chapter coming from a place of the Joy I live, gifted to me amid all the healing.

My gratitude is full to overflowing from the One within.

The greater energy of Oneness steps forward to support and give me encouragement.

It is a Presence that is with me when I focus my attention to being here and now.

It is the Loving that is the Truth of Me, and I just want to be thankful.

It is the living of me that didn't know I could survive.

My intention becomes clear, and I write.

I want to express my gratitude for being here to tell it.

It is the living and the stories I tell that arouse a shimmer of energy to share the miracle of finding life renewed.

I reach in to share the journey of this transitioning with those near and dear to me. First was my daughter of eleven years who departed three years after my father at fifty nine years, through all of the dimensions of grieving as years passed.

Then twenty-four years later as Mom passed with dementia and ultimately with Alzheimer's.

At this time I cared for my husband in his six-month process of transitioning with cancer.

This second journey very different than the first,
With the gift of healing from my inner awakening Presence
   with God.
A Journey to Behold! Just as I have been held, I hold the loving
   as I share it with you.
Be, that it might lift and hold you as I have been held
In this body, in this lifetime and into this and every next moment.

CHAPTER 4

Returning to Work

In a couple of weeks' time I returned to work where I could function as me without the constant pain of being without Emily and looking for her, getting her off to school, wanting to see what her needs were, and hearing her excitement for the day ahead. I needed to get back to familiar territory where I had functioned without her presence.

I discovered that the shock of this sudden death had taken a toll. I knew the faces of the people around me but, I couldn't remember their names! It was a desperate sensation, and it was embarrassing. These were people I had worked with for years now, and I just couldn't say their names as I met them. I knew the children and their names, but not my peers. I was aware of them watching me and not knowing what to say or how I was handling living. I could hear their sorrows and thoughts saying inwardly. It saddened me to bring this fear up in others. People turned from me with their hidden tears, while mine dripped down my face. I cried going to work and driving home. I cried when I arrived home until I wore myself out and went to bed with pillows surrounding and hugging me.

In the morning, I awoke with the alarm clock set to the classical Christian radio station and waited for words from God that would engage me enough to lift myself out of bed. I held on to them as they came through in some way each day and proceeded to a schedule of dressing and eating something for breakfast. Sometimes I ate alone but mostly I would go next door with Emily's best friend, Alicia, and my friend, her mom, Sheila. I would fix a bowl of cereal and a drink of juice or coffee and carry it out through the backyard to their back door and into their kitchen. I sat at their table as Jimmy got off to work, and the kids got up for school. I got to listen to the sounds of their day, and it gave me some sense of belonging. It gave me someone to speak to, to check in with, and watch Alicia go off to school. It got me out the door to move into this next day.

Soon, I turned to and spoke with Ebony, the black cat, and Penny, the copper colored dog who also kept me going in the morning. Ebony almost always talked back with her *meow, meow*ing, while Penny just wagged her tail, carrying Emily's sock in her mouth. Every day she would run and jump to the top of Emily's bed, asking daily where she was. The loyalty and joy of this companion-in-waiting sent me to painful episodes and bouts of wailing—a frequent part of my days.

Soon after I returned to work, the child with cystic fibrosis was again hospitalized, as often happened with these children who needed frequent medical attention. I was happy to see Christopher. He had come back into his body on August 11, and now he was here for me to embrace! We were right in the center of the pediatric unit at the T of the three hallways where the playroom and the main desk for gathering was located. It was an extraordinary event as we greeted each other. He seemed as happy to see me as I was to see him. It was then as we held each other that I became aware that even though we greeted in the middle of the busy intersection in the center of our pediatric unit—no one was there, just Christopher and me. He smiled and reached up for me, and I stooped down so we could put our arms around each other. I held him as if he had been born again. I was so grateful for his return.

And then … I felt the strength of something more in his embrace. I was no longer holding him; *he* was holding *me* with a knowing and reassurance that I couldn't fathom in the moment. It was just clear that he knew, and he was holding me longer and more enduringly than I would or could have asked for. Our hearts held a joint understanding, I felt what he knew and had experienced. He had been there, out of his body, as Emily had left hers. Christopher had returned, and now he gave me his knowing. The wisdom in his eyes and the warmth in his arms and in his barrel-chested body were my sustenance and strength. In that moment he shared with me the courage of his returning.

The Light that surrounded us in that embrace formed an aura of calm and peace of the Comforter that arrived in the Loving Spirit of this child. The hallway in the middle of the pediatric unit remained totally clear and uninterrupted as this event took place. My heart was filled with awe and gratitude as I experienced it, and I can easily say that to this day I have this awareness and sense of knowing that God showed up in those moments that existed outside time.

My co-workers were very gracious to me. My dear friend Maggie, who drove me to the ER that afternoon, told me, "Judy, I know you can't be all here with us yet, but I am grateful for the part of you that is here." I felt an incredible acceptance of my process and felt the hearts of others reaching out to me. They weren't necessarily able to approach me, but they felt my sensitive presence. I walked through the day, attending to the children who were admitted. Being there was a space where I could function in my professional career as one would on any normal day. Being with the children was a place of belonging that I was familiar with.

A Story In Waiting / I Cried Out

There is a story that is calling to be written,
A story that has been growing in my life since when?
When was that?
Was it when Emily passed suddenly while playing at soccer camp,
Or was it since Mom and Dad joined to create my presence,
Or maybe and even before that as I waited to come into this body:
To experience a new way, a new learning for expressing and
Expanding into greater elevations of my Soul?
But in this lifetime, the greatest wake-up call came
That eleventh day in August 1983 when
Emily did not return home from soccer camp.
The phone call arrived at the hospital where I was with the children,
Hearing that she was not breathing
And all resuscitation efforts were being made.
This man with a gentle voice spoke it without using the "D" word.
Saying that she was at their facility and "all efforts were being made."
My mind began to whirl and my body reacted with pure
attention to possibility.
Who would say these words to me? This must be a mistake.
"You know that I love the children, God. Why, what, where, who is this for?
Please, God, please, don't take mine from me! Not mine."
That was the beginning of the Greatest Learning in this lifetime,
The greatest lesson, which became my "Letting Go and Letting God."
Finding that all my gifts and abilities were not even a portion
Of what it would take to keep her life here in her sweet body
Delivered through my womb.
Helplessly, I cried out,
"Where is this Living to be found now??
Where did I go wrong? What did I, didn't I do?"
This beautiful soul that taught me *joy* and had given me
The greatest experience of living I had known in this lifetime.
How would I recover the *joy* that she brought me and taught me

So willingly and unceasingly?
Looking without answers, seeking and not finding.
Was she even really here?
That question haunted me with the shock of it.
My mind could not wrap around this potential for loss.
My body went numb as I cried out to find her
And know where she was and how I could be there with her.
My heart, though pierced with pain, walks the journey ….
JmB (2012)

CHAPTER 5

Searching

All the while, I began my search for Emily and her new whereabouts. The need to search was a strong force from within, particularly while I was at home. My arms tingled, even painfully, as I ached to hold her, touch her, and cuddle her as I had done since her birth. On autopilot, I looked for her to care for her, to wake her in the morning. Surely, this was all a dream, an unreal big mistake, and she would be coming around the corner or out of her bedroom at any moment. I sensed her presence as if she had just appeared as usual, but each time, my body would ache from her absence.

God and I were not finished with this serious and sincere endeavor that needed to be worked out. My mind was obsessed with the need to see Emily again. I cried out to God in countless ways to ask what this was about and where Emily was. Giving up my job as mom to Emily was insurmountable, and I needed assurance she was being cared for in heaven as I'd studied and believed about it.

Now I wanted to *know* it in a *real* way. Emily was my only child, and having been a single parent, I was now on my own, living by myself at our Timber Oaks address. We had attended church together where I was a choir member, and being in early preschool child-care together, we'd done a lot of singing there on Sundays and weekdays. As I asked where she was, often a song would come to my awareness. I would hum and listen to the words for some comfort and reassurance. The words of the songs were always an inspiration for me, and I heard:

> Jesus Loves Me, this I know.
> For the Bible tells me so.
> *Little ones to Him belong.*
> They are weak but He is strong.
> Yes, Jesus loves me! Yes, Jesus loves me!
> Yes, Jesus loves me! The Bible tells me so.

Emily had sung this song so many times that at her funeral service our organist used the piano to play an extended and eloquent version. She told me the song was originally inspired by the loss of a child. I played it over and over to myself in my heart and in my mind. I needed the reassurance of continual Loving for Emily and myself, as I'd known it in our life together. I needed to hear God's Presence was with me.

Another song came during the first Christmas Holiday:

> Away in a manger, no crib for a bed,
> The little Lord Jesus lay down His sweet head.

I kept singing to find a message for me as the words moved on. It came in the second verse:

> Be near me, Lord Jesus, I ask thee to stay
> Close by me forever, and love me, I pray.
> *Bless all the dear children in thy tender care,*
> *And guide us to heaven, to live with thee there.*

Once again reassured, I began to research the scriptures for references to heaven. I found many references of God being out there and heaven being up there, but the way to being there I read was that heaven is a place within. That was *it!* I wanted to go there within, to be with her. I wanted to go too!

But, all the pain lingered on and felt very punishing. *This was truly a mistake. It surely can't be what God intends. God's love doesn't feel like this.* My mind obsessed over this part of me that hungered for her presence. I therefore concluded that since God had delivered this precious presence of this child to be with me as her mom, then surely I wasn't to be separated from her. I too was ready to stop the life in this body and pass to the other side to be with her so as not to have abandoned her and left her at camp when she needed me; that was my fear and my tremendous guilt. Somehow I hadn't done something that I should have; I hadn't cared for her adequately, hadn't seen a need of hers, hadn't been attentive. I wanted so badly to do it all over again with a different result. I could have kept this from happening—anything but dying! It was unbearable not to be able to do that and redraw this picture. I chose then to catch up with Emi, to complete my contract with God as her mom. I planned what drug I would use and how I would be successful at it. My nursing education gave me the information. I had a plan that, on one level, I knew was on purpose, ordained by God, for the loving continuation of my life with hers!

Simultaneously, and on another functional level, I continued to listen to the contemporary Christian radio station where my alarm was set to get me out of bed each morning. I would ask, "Please tell me something, God, that I know is from You to me. I need something to find the strength and courage to face this day." Over and over I asked … and then I'd hear a verse or a word from a song, a message of reassurance. I received it, from God to me, and I'd get up.

Penny, Emily's golden cocker spaniel, would come to me every day, still carrying the remains of Emily's sock in her mouth.

Ebony, our black kitty would "talk" to me. I fed them, and we would talk about Emily not being here, yet again on this day.

I had to depart and gather myself in the car and again the tears would roll down my face as I felt the abandonment of parenting my child. I wanted to leave and be with her. It had been weeks since she had died. I had tried to direct myself into my former activity and that weekend I went to my exercise class at the complex behind my home. I rode my bike down the well-worn path that Emi and I had traversed many times and tried to get into the exercise regime. I could tell the others were surprised to see me. Again people were without words and didn't know what to say to me.

I was happy to leave and return to the open field toward our home. Out there in the open field, with a suffering heart I began calling out loud to God: "Please, God, let me see her one more time." I had read and knew it was possible. People had written of it. Others talked about the experience of seeing their loved ones after death. I had several books under my bed of these stories, and now I was wailing with tears. I cried out to God over and over, "Please, God, let me see her one more time! Please, God! Right here and now, in this open field!"

Without an answer once again, despite my wailing and sobbing, I walked my bike toward my house. I looked up and saw my mom approaching! She came running into the field to find me. "Why didn't you call me? Why didn't you call me?" she cried.

"But Mom! You're here! You're here, Mom! I needed you right now, and you are here!" I wailed with the exasperation and exhaustion of my emotions. She held me, her tears joining mine. We cried together for the first time since Emi's death.

She had gotten a phone call from the Christian Psychiatric Hospital where I had worked formerly for many years. One of the therapists that I knew and worked with had heard of Emily's death. A woman with my name had called and said that she wanted to kill herself and asked for help. I knew there was another woman with my name from the years when Emily's father and I lived near them. Her husband was a basketball player at the college there, and we were often teased about it. They were in fact "Chuck and Judy" with the same last name as ours. I said, "Mom, that wasn't me. I did not make that call."

My neighbor friend, Sheila, who guided my mom to my whereabouts, was with her, and I could clearly see that they didn't believe me. We went inside the house, and I told them what had happened that morning. I then called the facility to talk with the therapist there. I thanked him for the call, thinking of my need as well, and then made him promise to find the other woman with my name. I knew she was there and thought she must have called out for help.

I didn't actually get a call back with further information, nor should I have. Confidentiality would not have allowed it. I was just sure of her presence and of mine, and at that point my mother was called and appeared just in the moment of my own need and distress. Other things like this happened. I would think of someone I would like to contact, and they would call within minutes to see how I was doing. "I was just thinking of you and thought I would call," they'd say.

I don't know of the time span of this last occurrence alongside my plan to take my physical life. It was months in the planning when I knew the pain was more than I could endure. And one day it was clear that I should complete my plan to take my life. I was determined. I knew what I wanted. I wanted to be with Emily. It was also what God would want for us, to be together and one with Him. It was totally rational from my perspective. I knew the way, and I saw myself with her. That day, in my car, on my way to work, as tears flowed down my face, the music on WCSG began to play. I listened, and it was as if my Soul brought me to attention. I knew this song. I had sung it many times, and now I heard the words *for me! They were magnified, and I could feel the Presence of them:*

> Because He [God] lives, I can face tomorrow,
> Because He lives, all fear is gone.
> Because I know, I know He holds the future,
> That LIFE is worth the living, just because He Lives!

I knew this song. I had sung it many times before, but this time it was new again! Could that really be true? All *fear* is gone? I had become utterly fearful, more than I had ever known before. The living God could release *all* fear?

The words went on ….

"Because I *li i ive* … a Light of knowing encircled me."

My arms weakened, and I pulled off the freeway to sob! This was a message about living! Living here *now* was what I was supposed to do. Daily God had spoken to me in clear messages to get me to this day, and this was *the* Message of truth and the message of Life. It was for me today!

The message of this song was clear. Somehow the suffering would be attended to, and I would see what life held for me! God's Presence would continue to hold me! I would *stay*. I would go on *living*.

So with God's help showing up so clearly, I returned to the freeway and moved on to work. I continued to watch and seek, ask and listen. I wanted to know and have eternal life *with* my daughter. With God's Presence, as was just shown to me, I would find and *know* it. I did not want to wait to see her someday after I died. I wanted to see her now. Now, I had hope.

I struggled with the church that I and Emily had attended for years. Other adults and children were suffering because of Emily's death and what we had all gone through. Another of Emily's best friends attended with us there at Twin Lakes. She and other children wondered if they could die at camp like Emily. A counselor in the church offered support, and a grief and healing class was held. At one point I bolted from that class when I became the center of the gathering. It was too focused on me and my pain, and I stood up and said I needed out. I couldn't breathe and wanted to escape from all I was hearing.

I decided to attend church differently. I wanted to know if God was ever present in all of the local churches. Was God showing up for others as He was for me? I began visiting all of the churches in my city, and my question was the same: "Is God's Loving here?" In some places people knew me and had children who went to school with Emily. I was always welcomed in some way, and then, as I listened; I would hear the verse, the song, the message and know God was present. I heard the omnipresence of God. How did that work? How was it brought out and into our knowing experience? It was different in each place, but I knew it when I heard it. Sure enough. I asked. I listened. I heard. *God is Love. And it is here.* Thank You, God, for showing me. Thank you for trusting in me. For-giving me.

CHAPTER 6

Extraordinary Events

I worked one evening a week holding a support program with the children and families at the hospital. We held our gathering in the parents' lounge just outside the pediatric unit. Parents were invited who had children on the unit at the time. Often there were parents there who came in and knew of my loss. It was delicate for me to be their support, when I knew they were also being a support for me. It meant that I left work late in the evening. I left the city and got onto the freeway to the outskirts where I lived with tears flowing as usual.

It was late when I pulled into my driveway on a clear evening. I climbed out of the car, again calling out to God for comfort. I reached up into the sky as if reaching to heaven as I called out, "Please, God, give me strength!" With a weakened and exhausted body I simply fell to the ground on my hands and knees onto the rocky surface. I didn't want to go into the empty house without her again.

In that moment of sadness, I felt a Presence surrounding me. I looked up to see what it was. It seemed the starry sky dropped down, and I was enveloped as I sat there. I recalled from the scriptures something about a firmament of the heavens. I felt the stars lowering like a dome, and I was lifted from my sorrow. In the Presence I was not alone. I was awestruck and felt the comfort of it. I received of it, lifted myself up, and drove the car into the garage. I entered the house where Penny and Ebony greeted me, and we slept peacefully.

During this same period, my sister Pam called me to ask how to help Rick, my nephew. She told me that Rick was having dreams every night where Emily, his sister Stephanie, and he were riding bikes faster and faster down the road. He would awaken upset and tearful. I responded, "How wonderful that he gets to see her! Tell him to have fun on his bike ride with Emily. Let him know it's okay to see her and be with her in his nighttime." I had not yet dreamt of her after her passing and longed to see her or have the chance to talk with her. Rick was spending every night with her. Once he knew it was okay, I was told, the dreams ceased.

After a time—I can't tell you exactly when—I did start to have some dreams. I had always dreamt with some consistency and welcomed this visitation with my nighttime sleep. The first one that stood out was a time when I was studying the verses about heaven from the scriptures and was reminded of the mansion of many rooms being prepared for us. It is said, "In my Father's house are many rooms; if it were not so, I would have told you. I am going there to prepare a place for you. And if I go and prepare a place for you, I will come back and take you to be with me that you also may be where I am." It is prefaced this way: "Do not let your hearts be troubled. Trust in God." (See John 14:1-3)

The mansion I am speaking of is a reference that I had sung about many times that referred to this portion of verse. I had a dream of visiting this mansion, the one I had heard and read about. I had arrived and searched down the hallway through the rooms of many colors, among them royal deep reds and purples and rich, lush greens, in velvet and satin with gold trim. I was there searching for Emily. I wanted to find her as I walked through the hallways of this royal premise. Was she here just as I'd heard and been told?

Just then I heard her voice, "I am here, Mommy! I'm here!" I had entered this mansion as promised by God and heard her voice. It was Emily's voice, and I knew her. I sensed her presence, though I did not see her then. I bolted from the vision and from her sweet voice. I knew as I awakened that her presence had been bestowed upon me and mine to her! It lifted me to tears of relief. It gave me assurance that God—the eternal source of life—and I had found inner communion. It felt elegant and peaceful, and Emi's voice was joyful and reassuring. I had the experience of oneness with her voice and a sense of union, of being in this place together even if only for a short period. It was joyful for me to know! I was so excited to hear her voice and to be able to recall what I had just experienced. I have carried this with me over time with great gratitude and comfort for our visitation.

But other dreams, repeated over the years, were not as comforting. They were dreams of being in a home—sometimes the same home with the familiar rooms where Emily and I lived. I would move through the kitchen and living room and bedrooms and always the toys that were Emily's things. I would search and find her and then wonder where I had been. Where had she been? I hadn't seen her for a while, and I would reprimand myself for not caring for my daughter. Why wasn't I caring for her? Who had cared for her in my absence?

Then she would appear, and I would in some way attend her. I didn't always see her, but I could sense her being present and with me in some way in the house. We would have a busy time of catching up, always ending with my sadness at not attending to her and caring for her as I should be. This dream continued intermittently throughout the coming years.

Meanwhile, I also found more guidance and answers for myself from a group of people who gathered to find God's presence from within. Throughout my religious upbringing in my family church, I had often asked about the walk with Christ since I had accepted Jesus into my heart. Why aren't we talking about what we do now as we are living this choice throughout our daily and weekly life? I wanted to talk about and learn how to walk the experience with understanding as was told by the life of Jesus the Christ. I didn't get much response at my church at that time.

So I asked elsewhere. I had found that heaven is a place within—that I could go there and be there also. I wanted to learn how to be with the living presence of Christ eternally and not wait until I died to see my daughter again. I wanted to know how to be there *now from within* as it was written and thrive with awareness of an eternal existence. I met some people who told me about Insight Trainings, which led to other friends who told me about a church called the Movement of Spiritual Inner Awareness or MSIA.

As soon as I heard the name, I said, "That's where I want to go. My daughter lives there, and that's where I want to go. How do I get there?" I began to attend their group meetings to find the guidance I was looking for. There were weekly and weekend events, and at one point there was a retreat for a weekend, called "Going to Heaven Within." Wow! I was in the right place. During that weekend Emily came to me and we interacted every night in some way. Sometimes there was just some looking and knowing without words. Other times it was as if we had continued on as normal with her growing. It was as if she was keeping me abreast of her status. My nighttime heavenly travels began to grow.

CHAPTER 7

Investigation to Discovery

What was the process of my recovery, and how would I cope? There were so many missing pieces. What had actually happened to Emily, and who was there who might have helped her? *What will I do next to care for my missing child, and how will I get some answers for my own peace of mind and heart?* I needed to know.

I was met with a great deal of secrecy from the camp where Emily had been. No one would speak to me regarding what had happened with Emi before she passed, for fear of a lawsuit. It was disheartening to me to have no one share with me the situation and condition of my daughter on the days before her passing. The very people who were with her last, seemingly caring for her safety and comfort, were the very people who would not, could not, and were advised *not* to speak to me!

Who was caring for her? How did that take place, or why did it *not* take place? *What happened?* It was a devastating feeling to be unable to pick up my daughter from where I'd left her at soccer camp, with some of her best friends, to enjoy one of her favorite activities. And now … *she's not there where I left her, nor is she here … with me … her mom … who cares for her.*

I had to go through state protocol to request a legal hearing with the people who'd attended Emily to meet and ask my questions.

I got assistance and filed the papers to create this audience. The time was set up, and we met at Camp Wakeshma with the camp director, who was also the principal of a local elementary school, a college student who was Emily's cabin counselor, her soccer coach (who was the mother of one of the counselors who performed CPR on Emily), and the state representative for camp regulations and guidelines.

I did come to the meeting with the report that through extensive autopsy, there was *no* clear cause of death. Lab reports of blood tests, including presence of drugs or other possible toxins, all came back negative. The ER room physician director, who was also the County Medical Examiner, assured me that the extensive autopsy, which he personally oversaw, was as thorough as he could make it. He, too, wanted to know what could possibly have happened. He also let me know that he was available for me to talk and ask questions as often as I needed. I did that, meeting with him three times thereafter.

I researched, and I met with our pediatricians where I had been a full-time staff member for a couple of years on the pediatric unit. They were devastated over the loss. We met to inquire and try to explain what could have occurred. I asked questions and listened while they quested and pursued information amongst their expertise. I asked to hear the ways that might comfort me with my fears and guilt, but also to find for all of us who care for children what this could have been. We met and asked, "What could have happened? What created such a sudden unforeseen event?"

Emily had experienced a block-out of breathing and functioning while being admitted to the hospital for scarlet fever more than two years earlier. A heart block is an event identified by loss of respirations and heartbeat. She was treated on the pediatric unit where I worked. The meeting with the pediatricians after her death was one of disdain, accusation, guilt that was sideswiped, and sorrow! The guilt of this sudden death of a seemingly healthy child lay all over us. I realize that this meeting with them gave me some source of support, even though no resolution came from it.

The incident of her heart block was implicated in the autopsy. The medical examiner referred me to the leading national research director who had executed this research in Florida for sudden infant death syndrome (SIDS). I was familiar with SIDS from my experience and education as a pediatric nurse. I then asked to have her slides and reports sent to this facility, and the SIDS researcher consented to evaluate the information that had been gathered. He called me shortly after receiving the pathology reports and history, and we talked. He made clear his opinion that the scarlet fever event had not affected the heart tissue as he saw it and added that there was only healthy heart tissue evident. He also added that sudden death syndrome, while it peaks at four months of age, never drops back down to zero.

As I listened and watched over the years, and from the newspapers and media reports, I've noticed this for myself. I'd heard and read articles relating how teens and young adults were engaged in athletic activity and suddenly fell over without evident cause. I wasn't alone, looking at and experiencing this sudden loss. If there was no physical evidence of such a sudden and frightening event, then what did happen? I've continued asking.

So now, back to the first meeting, with the camp staff, to find what more could be gathered. It was very emotionally and spiritually important to me that the people who last cared for my daughter tell me of how they cared for her. To have no one speak to me after the death of my child left me overwhelmed with desperate questions. What could they do now? What had been done? It was time for me to hear how she had been attended to. Who was in attendance when it occurred? Did they see it coming or not? What had preceded this sudden fall? How did they respond? Who held a close watch, and how was it executed? And regardless of all that, I also wanted mostly to know whether they had prayed for her. Had they asked for God's guidance? Had they held her in His loving hands?

After being in the emergency room with Emily and the staff there, the camp staff had escorted me to get her belongings at the camp. I remember picking them up but don't recall exactly how or when that happened. What stood out was that her sleeping bag had been rolled up and passed on to me, and when I got home, I found that her sleeping bag was soaking wet with urine! No one said anything to me about this. Emily had not wet the bed for years. She did have events of bed-wetting up until seven years of age, and I was told from a medical evaluation (a sleep study) that she simply slept very deeply and wet herself without being aware of a signal from her bladder. She also drank a great deal like her father, and now there was a large deposit of urine in the sleeping bag, just as in years before. This was now four years later. What happened that she had this incident? Why didn't she call me? What was she intending to do? Was someone helping her? The amount of urine and the smell of it was pervasive!

Developmentally, with all of her growth as a preadolescent, I had been aware of her changes at eleven years. She was now wearing her first bra and had had her third menses. She had grown about five inches that year, and the leaps in her ballet class with the growth of her long legs were a beautiful sight to behold. She also played soccer whenever she could and become her team's star goalie with her height and strong kick. I knew that preadolescence was a very private time because of all the bodily and emotional changes as well as the hormonal stimulation, and she would not have wanted to bring attention to her newly growing body. She was ahead of most of her peers, and she would hide her issues as best she could.

I reflected. What had I missed? Who would tell me? The detective and the nurse researcher in me were energized by the desperate need I felt to take care of my daughter. *I am her mom, and I will seek and find.* I asked God to direct my search with full knowing, and with diligence, I would find the way of knowing as well.

So at the meeting with the state representative and the camp staff; the director, the cabin counselor and the soccer coach were all in attendance. The health coordinator on staff, who I learned was a premed student, was not present.

The mom who was Emi's coach, with her son and another camp counselor who performed the CPR, also attended Emily's funeral. I had met them. It was difficult for all of us. I saw and felt their numbness and helplessness with me and also for this experience. We were all in shock as Emily's body lay near us in the all-white casket. The mother-coach let me know that the boys were having a hard time, but they wanted to come to let me know of their sorrow for me and their failed efforts. We looked with deep compassion into each other's eyes, knowing the pain that was there without words. I hugged them for their efforts; they were the last people who had embraced my daughter as they persevered to resuscitate her. They were the ones designated to bring back the breath and life of Emily. It didn't work.

(An additional irony of this situation was that while working in pediatrics, I, too, had to learn an advanced form of CPR called advanced life support. In fact, I had just been recertified on August 10, 1983, the day before the event with Emily at camp. Why didn't it work? I had posed this question to our pediatric nurse educator who coordinated this training. I learned that at best, this service is only 30 percent successful.)

I could only be ever so grateful that they were at her service within the moment when she fell over. They sustained her until the emergency squad arrived from a nearby hospital a few minutes later. There were no words to speak. I could only thank them with tears in my eyes, knowing that in some way they had held her after her last breath to give a breath to her when she could not do it for herself. They were there when I was not. My loving gratitude was and is unceasing for those moments and their gift to her and to me.

I had heard from some of her cabin mates, including Molly,

who was one of her best friends, as well as Amy and Rachel. Their moms had rushed to camp that same day and then to the hospital where I was with Emily. They also shared with me in my shock and numbness of this reality. They and other classmates and parents came to the funeral home. Some brought the last pictures they had taken of Emily to show me the fun they were having together while at camp. Another shared that Emily had borrowed a pair of soccer socks. I had not packed her socks! She wanted them back to have something from Emily. Through the rush of events in the ER to care for Emily, I had only found one to return to her.

Again with fear and trepidation, we gathered at this meeting with the soccer camp that Emily had chosen to attend. So what did the people here have to share with me? It was clear that since there was no cause of death from all the autopsy reports, I would not have evidence to file a lawsuit for negligence, which I had already declared I would not do, so now these people were free to speak with me.

They expressed their sorrow and wanted to include me in the process that they had initiated to assist the children after her departure. The incident had happened on a Thursday, and camp was still in session. Her cabin counselor wanted to take me to Emily's cabin. Her counselor pointed out where she bunked and that she had bunked next to her. She then wanted me to see all of the notes that were written to her on the walls and bunks after their supportive sessions with counselors after they learned what had happened to Emily. Their fears were being attended to, and this was one measure of speaking to their friend who had passed. They wrote notes to Emily of their love and joy and admiration of her. It was very touching to read their words that would be there for years to come. Perhaps all this attentiveness had came for children in the future and their secret developmental safety needs.

We rejoined the others and sat for further discussion. I asked them to tell me more of what had happened. Why hadn't Emily called home for some help about her sleeping bag? Her counselor did not seem to be aware of my discovery, even though she had shown me that she slept next to her. Why wouldn't she have called me? I then learned that phone calls were allowed only in an emergency. What would an emergency have been? How would the campers have known what would qualify? Her counselor and the director told of Emily having complained of a headache for about twenty-four hours prior to collapsing and that she went to the health staff where she had been given one tablet of Tylenol to assist her on three occasions. The health staff person was not there to talk further about this headache and one Tylenol.

Emily's coach stated that on the day of her passing, it was her turn to serve in some way in the dining room, and she had been cheerful. Also that day, there was an inspection of sorts, and they had a longer lunch period. After serving and returning to their cabins for quiet time, she'd slept. Upon rising and heading for the soccer field she had greeted her coach and said, "Today we are going to have a great game!"

The campers played on a field that was partially dug out from the hillside that overlooked the lake. It was a lovely site. I imagined them running back and forth, connecting with the ball as the opportunity came, moving among her teammates as I had seen her do many times. It was a beautiful setting. They proceeded to tell me that on August 11, 1983, she took her turn in line for the drill, and as she kicked she fell over onto the ground. Her coach was at hand and moved to her side to ask if she was okay. She didn't respond. She called for her son, who was nearby on the playing field with another group. Within a minute he went ahead with CPR. They called 911.

In my materials, I have a more complete version from a parent and the information she gathered from some of the camper friends. It states:

Two days prior to Emily's death she awoke very ill. She told Rachel, her friend next to her, "My head hurts so much that I can't move it on my pillow." She complained of dizziness but was without a stomach ache or fever. She vomited in the breakfast line, and Kathy took her to the Health Officer. He gave her one Tylenol and sent her on her way. She rested and wanted to play. Five times the log states Emily returned for help with her headache that continued. Angie says it was six, because she went with her the night before the log states, when the headache began. The coaches kept telling her she could sit out and watch … she did that too. Her teammates say she was grabbing her head and her stomach that morning as she tried to play. Natalie saw her on the ground and came to help her up after most of the others were gone. "I blacked out for a few seconds," said Emi. "But don't tell anyone. You know, my dad nearly died once when he had an appendix operation, and I died once too when I was in the hospital for scarlet fever. My papa died, and we buried him." *"Emily, why are you talking about dying?"* her friends wondered. "Well, if you die, we'll bury you in your soccer clothes!" they answered in humor.

Emily did not call home. The camp neither encouraged such calls nor clarified how to make them, as I heard it. What would an emergency be to a young preadolescent? How would she execute her request while being surrounded by her peers, not wanting to feel embarrassed? Her counselor lay in the bed right next to her and in the middle of the cabin. Did she not notice the odor or Emily's discomfort? How does a preadolescent child decide any given "emergency" means she should call home? What constitutes an emergency? She had attended camp earlier that year with our church association, and it was made clear that any child could call home. Just ask your counselor and you would be guided to do so, with the support of your counselor.

In our meeting the conversation was laden with sorrow and guilt. And yes, truly yes, with tears in their eyes, they had all prayed fervently for Emily to resolve. The director, who was also an elementary school principal, said he questioned his professional worthiness. The counselors were all young adults, and their goal seemed to be to get the campers past Wednesday, the peak of homesickness. (This was one of the sentiments I heard many times from other families who had severe health incidents with their children at camp.)

There were two adults overseeing how many campers? And the counselors were young college-age adults having a fun summer job. What was their level of attentiveness? How much did they know about the growth and development of this age group? And where was this premed student who was being extensively educated to observe physical status and make a diagnosis? I still wanted to hear from him. When would I hear from him and learn what his observations were?

Let me insert at this point: Although a physical exam and assessment would have once been required, it was no longer required by the state guidelines. We had been informed of this. However, I had one done anyway. Because of experience over two years earlier with what they called a heart block from the scarlet fever diagnosis, I wanted a good physical. We made an appointment with our group of pediatricians and we set up a thorough and extensive exam from the nurse practitioner. Emily allowed this loving woman to ask lots of questions regarding her health and examine her body with all the changes coming into adolescence. I got to be the mouse in the corner listening to an educational dialogue between my daughter and another adult. I was glad and reassured by this measurement of her health. But when we took her to camp, I had forgotten to bring this paperwork, which I'd intended to turn in.

CHAPTER 8

Other Factors

Emily spent the week before camp with her dad and went on vacation with his girlfriend to announce their engagement to Emily and her two sons. As they departed, I could see Emily retreating from these boys in the back seat. They were near her age, but not having the one-to-one attention from her father was a new experience.

She and her dog, Penny, had just come back from a 4H dog competition, Emily with an elegant hairdo that was a very large braid encircling the top of her head. Upon the undoing of her hair we'd discovered that there were open sores on her scalp that needed treatment, and while being with her dad she would need to ask for help from her dad or his fiancée. I didn't know if that ever happened. Later, at the funeral home, when I asked, they looked at each other blankly. That was my answer.

Emily's hair was extremely thick like her father's. It was very straight and hung to her hips. Caring for it was a task we handled together, especially since she was clearing dandruff. We were using a treatment shampoo. After the beauty shop put her hair up in a winding braid that she had seen in a magazine, it was up as long as she could leave it. In those three or four days, some sores developed. She needed help, and I knew it would be hard for her to ask. Did I tell her dad before they left? I believe I did.

But they had another agenda. They were letting her know that they were getting married and announcing their engagement to the children that week. It would have had a big emotional impact on Emily. After their return, Chuck never informed me, and Emi never talked of it. It was a pattern of her father, who was unwilling to communicate with me. I always had to dig. I think Emi would have tried to protect me from it and hold on to the disappointment of the reality of us never getting back together. We directed our two days together into getting her ready for camp.

Another psychosocial status was that Emily and I had been living with a partner of mine and his son for an entire year with the intention of marrying. Then, a month earlier, those plans had ended. He moved out. His son created so much stress for his father and me that it had come between us, and he just chose to leave one day. As a result of the loss of financial support for housing, I had met with a realtor gentleman, including Em in the discussion. I hoped we'd choose to move into a house next door that was a bit smaller and more affordable.

So her dad brought her home with his new development, my partner had left, a new home was in consideration, and we had two days to get ready for camp. Emily needed a new soccer pantsuit, shopping was in order, her hair and scalp needed care, and my uncle had been hospitalized. We planned to stop in to see him on our way to camp. I forgot to bring the physical examination report, and that became one big guilt: if I had brought it, would the camp have called me? One member not only said so but was bold enough to state that they would not have allowed her admission to camp.

This was a huge source of grief that held me guilty as not caring for my child—just more evidence that as a mom, who was trained as a psychiatric nurse and pediatric child life specialist with a master's degree in child human growth and development, I had failed. What happened? Was her heart just too heavy to stay and move through all that was upon us? I added up the elements of guilt as I gathered them. I ached with the thought of them. Was there physical truth in referring to someone as being heartbroken?

I begged to go back and do it over again. I pleaded. *Please, God! I didn't want it to happen this way! I didn't mean it! I didn't want to hurt my daughter! Please let me wake up and find this all a big dream! A fearful and awful unreal dream!* My suffering at this point was tight in my abdomen and excruciating to my thoughts and emotions. I could only cry out and cry within. Guilt settled in. It felt like a deep hole of blackness hovering over and around me—the one in front of me at the cemetery where my feet bolted from the fear of it. I sank into helplessness. Who now, what, would lift me from this desperation?

Finally, one day, the call from the medical intern student came. Was it a month later, two or three maybe? I remember where I was in the house. The phone was in the kitchen at the back of the house and had a long cord. The kitchen, a half bath, and my bedroom stretched along the rear of the house overlooking the yard and vacant field behind us. I listened intently, moving slowly back and forth in this space or sitting on the commode, to hear how he had attended Emily. He was more than apologetic as he described his observations, telling me Emily had described her headache to be at the back of her head and how as a new intern student he had serious concerns regarding three different scenarios. But then he had mistrusted his fears and brushed it off as some form of overactive imagination.

He cried and spoke at length of his feelings of guilt. He had sought out counseling to examine his own worthiness and choice of profession. I just kept breathing with tears of desire going down my own cheeks. I may have asked some questions, I don't remember, but he talked with me extensively. For an hour or two I spoke and listened with him. What could I say? I knew his helplessness and feelings of inadequacy. He must have spoken of her vim and vigor, her beauty and strength, her popularity with her friends, but a nagging headache was what she came to him about. She came to the clinic six times with this headache, and each time he gave her one Tylenol as he was allowed by the health guidelines for kids at camp.

I sank deeply into my sorrow. Emily didn't have headaches. If you were to ask me how often she complained of a headache, I would have to say that I don't even recall one. Why didn't she call? Did she ask to? Did she ask for me? Who was listening? Emily had a persistent headache at the back of her head for more than twenty-four hours before her fall. She had a fainting episode on the premises the day before without adult observation. Only her dear friend had seen it, and Emily insisted she was not to tell. She rested and slept deeply after lunch the next day to be ready to play. While sleeping she had a bed-wetting incident. Then she reached to kick the ball, fell over, and could not be resuscitated. The picture was clear as it was going to get for now.

I needed to take action. What could I do? I learned that staff members at the hospital where I worked were also listening and thinking. Someone encouraged me to inquire from our state legislator regarding what had happened. When I met with Our representative and she heard my story, she informed me that this year new regulations were to be written. The protocol was to rewrite the guidelines for camp every ten years, and I was encouraged to write about what would be needed to prevent this type of incident for families and kids of all ages.

I wanted to see this change. I wanted to create a format for safe care that was not clearly identified for her. I found that Maggie, our pediatric nurse educator amongst other nurse educators at Borgess were eager to help. They already initiated and created some guidelines that they saw should have existed or needed to be written. We rallied and wrote a petition listing the needed conditions to create physical and emotional safety. Copies were distributed and signed (see appendix #1).

An army of people stepped forward to sign this petition! They included all the people at the hospital who knew my story and didn't know how to speak to me. Parents who had stories of their children suffering at camp came forward to tell me their stories. Some wrote their stories to add to mine, and we sent them forward to submit to the state regulators for children at camp for all of Michigan. A news article had given us more attention, and more parents contacted me (see Appendix #2). The result was hundreds of signatures sent to the regulations committee.

The next thing I knew, one of our state senators wanted to know why there was so much clamor and invited me to a meeting at his office in Lansing. I was happy to accept this invitation and attend. I brought Maggie with me. We forcefully made our case and included many of the other stories. There were several listeners, including one man who persistently scoffed at our concerns and recommendations. But our voices were many, and many proposed regulations were incorporated, and guidelines were put on the agenda for camp counselor education.

I was then invited to the next couple of educational workshops to train counselors for the developmental and psychosocial needs of preadolescent children. I included the many reasons a child needed to be able to phone home and the value of having a physical history on hand that lists any idiosyncrasies of each child. (As I write this, I am reminded that the last movie that Emi and I went to was *E.T. the Extraterrestrial.* I remember E.T. himself requesting to "phone home!" and the eternal message, "I am right here," as he points to the center of his forehead.)

It is important to be aware of the sensitivity of the body identity changes and this preadolescent stage of secrecy. Campers need the reassurance of someone listening to their process with genuine interest and understanding. Emily had needed a safe opportunity to ask for help without being embarrassed around her peers. I had the rewarding opportunity with these young adults who wanted to be counselors and have fun with kids at camp to let them know of the kids' specific needs and issues. They needed to be looking and listening to what might be developing. Could they recall what it was like for them, be sensitive to needs for intervention, and trust a child's concerns as real and valid? I had the chance to represent the life of Emily as I knew her while proposing that my experience might help other children who wanted to have the joy of camp life. I was thankful as God gave me the courage to share my words to assist others so that their eyes and ears might be more aware to see and to listen. It was a lesson for me as well as for the young man who was the intern student and the director of the Emily's camp, as along with others who care for children. We all needed to find what each of us needed to learn.

All around me people sought counseling to cope with the fear of sudden unexplained death of a child while away at a camp setting. I heard stories of families who had their child at the camp and the ways that they chose to figure it out. Our church brought in counselors for her friends and peers. Some of these friends were with her at camp earlier in the summer. Parents needed to find a way to reassure their own children that they would not die if they wanted to attend camp.

I wanted to reassure children of their safety if they chose to have the fun experience of leaving home for a week at a camp without being disconnected from family. A safe place needs to be free of the fear of how others might value or hear them and free of the risk of embarrassment. For example, I learned that counselors at Emily's soccer camp made children jump off the diving board if they received a letter from home. Her friend Molly had told her about it before they attended, and Emily had told me.

As time went by, other people began coming up with ways to assist me. I began to realize that not only did I have my grieving to attend to, but I also needed to hear the ideas of certain people around me. A few inevitably asked, "Was she your only child?" or "Do you have other children?" I wanted to say, "Would that matter?" I didn't, but the thought was there that if I had other children, maybe it wouldn't hurt so much or be so terrible to deal with?

Other people simply avoided me. I sensed that I reminded others of a pain and hurt that they could not imagine, whether walking through the cafeteria to get lunch or regular gatherings with friends (which no longer happened). Some told me so and let me know of their prayers.

One group of caring women from Emily's school invited me to lunch to encourage me to quickly adopt a child, as one friend had done. It seemed like something one might do if their dog died, but I didn't feel I could replace my beautiful unique child by adopting another. This woman, who had done so, sat among us. As I looked at her, I saw no evidence of joy but rather of sadness at this added burden of misplacement for her grief.

Another woman from our church had two young sons. She was a single mom like myself, and many of us knew she was in therapy with our pastor. I had reached out to her, and now she asked me to please sign to be the guardian of her children should anything happen to her. As I gave this request some thoughtful attention, I learned that she had previously expressed the wish to die and attempted suicide in the past, and now with feelings of unworthiness, she felt that I would be more deserving of her boys than she. She wanted to lift my sorrow and move on to realize these former death attempts.

Others turned away with their sad helplessness. I knew of that helplessness too. I had helped others with their grieving and loss, and now I was in their place. Their helplessness was delivered to me, and now I would learn what it was like to step through it.

PART TWO

SELF CARE

CHAPTER 9

Caring for Myself

It felt strange to only have me to care about. There was an emptiness about it and always a feeling that there was something missing, someone I wasn't attending to. It was lonesome to care about myself, by myself. Something was missing, and I needed to fill that gap. It was deeply uncomfortable, and I often felt a quivering sensation in my body. It was like a realignment of sorts to get my nervous system on a new track for functioning. It was challenging for me to direct my attention to something other than my daughter and me.

The doctors and nurses who were close to me at the hospital checked in on me; was I eating, sleeping, getting out, or exercising? They gave me thoughtful words or even assignments to ease my pain. I have mentioned this previously, but the words and sincerity were deeply rooted and supportive for me. One carefully phrased word of support came from Maggie. She let me know that she knew that I wasn't all there with my daily job in pediatrics, but said, "We're thankful for that portion of you that can be here." She held my hands and said it directly to me with a loving focus of her eyes. I trusted the honesty and caring that she was extending to me and took it in. It became my focus.

One part of me could step into this job that I loved for all the ways that I could be with the children and their fears at the hospital; another part of me embraced the parents in supporting their children. Those parts of me could walk through the door and come to work in this precious place, but now I served and loved parents and children who often feared what I was passing through. I felt their eyes on me. I felt their hearts as they reached out with words of knowing and strength to enable me to move on. Maggie had given me a great piece of courage, and I would use it to grow and move forward. I feared that others would be wondering when I would shake it off or get over it, but this was a beautiful statement of acceptance and awareness, and I have always remembered it as an important point of reference.

One assignment for my reengagement of care with the children was with a delicately sweet and precious preschool child from Kenya, Africa, whose mother was a student at the local university. This little girl was in severe pain with sickle-cell anemia. As she wrapped herself around me and I put my arms around her, her pain seemed to cease, and she was able to rest peacefully and look around with interest at others and her surroundings. She had not been sleeping, and I had missed Emily's precious hugs. We just held on to each other. As she held on, I was being held. As I wrapped my arms and body around her, she was without pain. It was my privilege to care for her and hold her so endearingly, and she accepted and reciprocated. We nurtured each other into a place of heartfelt and physical healing. Her pain ceased, and my heart opened. We sat, rocked, and walked. She fell asleep, and I found an empty room with some open beds. I climbed onto a bed as we continued to hold one another and lay down with her, and I dozed off. I vaguely heard the doctors come in to check on her as we lay resting peacefully, and after a few whispers, they chose to move on and let us comfort each other. We each became the other's medicine and healing. The gift of it was more than precious. The Comforter of All Loving once again showed up.

This comfort became the path of my pursuit. And God was

my partner for a deeper level of knowing and understanding what this event was for in my life. I continued my search for more understanding. If life and death come from this eternal Source, then I intended to have more clarity with my inner questions. There must be a greater purpose and picture that I could find. I'd grown up trusting in God, but I was still reeling with shock and the inability to make sense of this traumatizing event in my life. I felt a fear such as I had never known before. It made me feel lost, fragmented, and foreign even to myself. All that I had known and learned up to now was not able to manage this fear that overwhelmed me. Others must be seeing this fear in my eyes and my demeanor.

I felt as though my sanity was on edge, and I asked for help in all directions. I went inside calling *in* to God and *out* to God with demands, asking what for and why. How could this have happened, and what was my role in all of this estrangement? I was searching inwardly but also feeling a huge separation outwardly that shook me with fear! The density of the pain felt like punishment, and I felt utterly abandoned and separated from God as a Loving Source.

I was focused intently on finding my daughter, and my greatest request was to see her again. I needed to connect the gap of separation from Emily with this fear of loss and separation from God. My focus was not to just believe in heaven and see her someday but to know *now* that she was being cared for. My child had been taken from me, and my job had been ended long before I was ready to let it go. There were all sorts of feelings rambling around inside. The fear brought up every troubling judgment that life could impose on me during this time, fear of separation and abandonment being the bottom line. The insecurity of it was sometimes disorienting. I lost time and had moments of not knowing who I was now.

I needed to find where the connection was for us to continue our existence. *"Please, God—let me see her again. If life is eternal, then let me see her.* I *need* this reassurance that her existence is real and that I can find life to go on." I kept breathing through the floods of tears, just kept breathing.

The nights were the hardest. Alone, I went to bed exhausted emotionally and mentally. I had worked as a psychiatric nurse therapist for many years, and with a wonderful facility just forty miles down the road, I often considered admitting myself to find escape. I did get into weekly counseling with a therapist I was acquainted with. She led me forward, and I felt her checking on my functional ability. I didn't hospitalize myself or use any drugs other than some melatonin or some valerian root tea for sleep. But weekly, she would write down an assessment of my current status and what I was to take forward from our session to the following week. I knew when I was to return and knew that I had a place to say whatever I wanted and be the only self that I could be. The agenda was wide open, and I could bring up any thoughts, concerns, or requests for help.

Each morning, my alarm awakened me to the contemporary Christian radio station. I would lie there with the full body pillow I was clinging to and speak quietly with God, my eyes closed in an effort to avoid seeing this next new day. I waited for some words through a song or verse being spoken that would lift and encourage me to get up. They always came. I heard them clearly when spoken, the ones that I was to hear to get myself up from bed and begin the day. They were words of God's love, offering strength, and would hold me in some way without doubt, showing me the Presence of something stronger than I could muster for myself. I moved from the bed. Penny greeted me with her loyal and happy wagging tail, and Ebony talked to me with her strength of *meows*, and we began the day.

A close friend came to live with me for a period of a few months before moving elsewhere. Soon after I found a lovely young woman who was a student at the local university to rent space in my home. It was welcoming to have another person in the household with me.

I don't have a clear image regarding my awakening into a greater awareness of God's Spirit being present with me, but I have repeatedly stated that I called out for help and the reassurance of Emily's whereabouts. There came a woman who heard of my calling out and asked to meet with me. She told me of studying *A Course in Miracles*, and as she spoke, I felt a sacredness within her. She spoke of the scriptures as I knew them, but in different words in which I sensed a natural comforting and love. I thought at the time that she must have been a representation of the Holy Spirit. *This must be what it's like to have the Holy Spirit speak with you.*

Her words describing God's love and assurance for both myself and Emily were simply more expansive than I had heard in my traditional church upbringing. It was refreshing, and my heart felt lifted. It was like a truth I had been waiting to hear. I can sense it as I write this. She invited me to some study meetings, and soon I was being invited to an introductory event for a workshop called Insight I: The Awakening Heart. It was a-six day event that was being held in my city, now five years after Emily had passed. More than two hundred attended, and as I walked into the room, the crowd at this first evening frightened me. I did not want to meet all these people!

I worked hard at emotionally and mentally going to work each day and was overcoming a shocking reaction I had experienced. The effect of Emily's sudden death seemed to create a neurological response that came out in the form of forgetting the names of the people that I worked with. I mentioned earlier that I could not recall the names of my peers and co-workers as I met them at the hospital. It was embarrassing, and I found myself withdrawing from nearly all socializing and from places where I had to meet and respond to others. I was able to ask my closest staff friends on the pediatric unit to help me, but this room of two hundred people was more than I wanted to take on. I wondered how

I had managed to get myself into this situation. I could have, would have bolted from the room, but the first process presented to us gave me the baby step forward that I needed. We stood, approached one person at a time, spoke with direct eye contact, and repeated a choice from among three comments as to our willingness to greet them. It felt safe and as I looked directly at them, one at a time, I found myself willing to try out what was offered. The result was that the atmosphere became safer than I had imagined it could. I didn't have to think, I could just do one statement or another.

Over the coming days, we were greeted with a format of mini-lectures, time for questions and sharing how the processes were going for us, group games to represent life situations, guided visualizations, and one-to-one processes. For a one-to-one exercise, we faced a partner, and the first person asked a short series of questions, while the second person simply answered with whatever came to them to say in response. The first person held a neutral loving presence and asked the question without participating with an engaging response to the content but simply allowing the second person their own process of awareness as to the content of the answers that unfolded.

One particular significant process occurred after a lecturette regarding being a victim of our circumstances. I heard the words and felt an anxious expectancy. I was sure that I would remain a *victim* of the pain of my daughter's death my entire life. I was really very certain of this inevitable circumstance. But a revelation occurred! I can't tell you the questions. I don't remember them, but I came out on the other end of the exercise lifted from the condition that I had labeled myself with. A relief came over me. It was probably the first time I took a clear look at the possibility of our two lives being actually two separate lives, though our closeness prevailed.

It was a realization that I was still here for her but also here for me. She was always a wonderful teacher for me and this was no different than what she had always been for me. It was a point of freedom for both of us. It was a knowing that I wanted to own and investigate further. Something magical was revealed, and I wanted more clarity and experience with it. I began to clarify for myself. There was a new knowing that I could claim as I risked opening my heart. I had come from a very self-protective position from fear after Emily's sudden death, that my heart needed some refurbishing. I was in need of some new heart energy and a safe place to open again.

From this moment I moved forward trusting that God was truly bringing me a greater vision than the restrictive pain of death. I had been lifted above to see from a greater, larger perspective. This opening told me there was more going on than my painful experience, which also belonged to a greater knowing and purpose. I was newly aware of being reassured of the eternal existence of my daughter's life. My job parenting her here had not been relinquished as I continued to process within, and the pain of punishment and judgment that I felt personally was not the final reality. It had to be something greater if I was to find the Love of God as I knew it from her gift of life with me. I was getting the glimpses of what I had been asking for. Something connected inside me that said, *Emily is still with me. She remains my teacher, and that loving that was always there was giving me a place of showing up.* What appeared was a glimpse of eternal existence!

I can now see that the energy that came into this heartfelt process was laced with a Loving Presence that myself and others came to see as we moved through the days that followed. There was a connectedness that began to weave itself within us, surrounding us with a myriad of experiences and designs of opportunities that were simply laid out for us to open to *It*. I came to know *It*, and my heart opened and found a place to trust again; releasing fear which transformed and gave itself into this new safe place. A crucial confidentiality was maintained within the group, and we evolved into a community of loving and listening to an accumulation of experiences that we could all identify with to some extent. All circumstances gave each of us awareness that we could all grow from. This status was the result of the guidelines that were offered:

1. Do not hurt yourself and do not hurt others. (This hurtfulness was expanded beyond the physical aspects of hurting self or others to embrace hurtfulness mentally with our words to others and to ourselves and emotionally with the emotional baggage we all claim.)

2. Take care of yourself, so then you can help take care of others. Caring for myself first became a learning that I could share, from a basis to give freely, not from a place of have to, ought to, or should do with shame attached, but from a joyful giving of service from an abundance of overflow. Wow, how gracious!

3. Use every situation for your learning, growth, and upliftment (using every situation for what I was here to learn, so that my growth could lift me to something greater than this restrictive emotional reaction that I was having). There had to be a truth here somewhere for me to claim. I was begging to learn what this was truly about. This pain could *not* be of God. *So where does it come from? Do I even need to know or can I transform it to something of my learning, something that grows greater than this meager understanding? Can it be lifted to a new vision? I am available for being lifted from this current restrictive existence, God. Show me the way.*

The next move was to immerse myself in the next workshop to see what could be accessible for me. It was called Insight II: The Opening Heart. My heart led me and called me into this next step. It was a smaller group—about forty people—and again a few days long, but it was to become a more in-depth and personally engaging experience. There was no hiding in this situation. We all became a canvas of our own vulnerability that was shared beyond words, but words had to be brought forward for us each to find our own truth. The exercises were more personally absorbing and with an intensity that allowed a deep release of old, useless thought patterns and a transformation to new truths of uplifting and loving self-awareness.

Two of the women attending this Insight II training stayed with me at my home during the training. Joann became a close friend and after the training, Joann told me her story and how she was guided there with all that she had been through in her life. She told me she was led to a weekly gathering called: The Movement of Spiritual Inner Awareness. The name grabbed my attention due to my study and searching for the heaven that I knew was a place within as I had learned from the Bible scriptures.

I wanted to know how to go there! I wanted to be there also with Emily. I looked for guidance to open to this place within me where we could greet and meet as "being in heaven on earth" that I had studied about. I had never heard anyone talk about how to get there. Here was the answer to my request: *to be guided spiritually to go within*. I knew that it was so because I had asked. The scriptures stated, "Ask and you shall receive; seek and you shall find" (see Matthew 7:7). I knew that I had asked, and now I was hearing that this would lead me to my *knowing* and *being* with this place of heaven within—this place where I could reside while still in this body and be with my daughter, Emily.

I asked how I could join in. She said the meetings were held two times a week, and the next meeting was that evening in just more than an hour. "Could we go now?" I asked. We got into the car, and we were on our way.

I pondered her story as she drove and felt as if I had heard a precious piece of scripture that was the telling of her story to find God. It was an intensive, painful, and personal story that ended in this joyful woman who is now a dear friend. I was on my way, and I would be lifted just as I felt she had been.

We walked into the home of Cleora Daily, who brought the Insight trainings and these seminars to this Kalamazoo neighborhood just off the freeway, where several others were gathered with this warm atmosphere. We called in the Light, that which is the presence of God through Christ and the Holy Spirit, and also prayed for the spiritual director who guided us in this process of awakening to ourselves as a Soul. He was at that time manifesting physical ailments in his body. He and other staff people were responsible for creating the Insight Seminars, and in deep gratitude for his offering for us all, I thrust myself within to visualize his healing and wellness. It was at that instant that I saw myself as an actual body of light merging with the "Light Body" that was the spiritual director, named John-Roger.

I startled at what I had just seen and experienced. I had entered into an awakening of something significant, something that had just happened to me as a Source of Light with another as a Source of Light. I had never experienced such a thing before, and I shared this happening with those around me. They assured me of my experience and said that almost everyone who engages with this inner movement church will have some sort of gift that aligned with their movement of growth, learning, and upliftment. This was mine. I wanted more of this inner awareness and experience.

I was guided to a course of practical readings called Discourses that were divinely inspired and written by John-Roger for the purpose of individualizing a study between the participant and God. I signed up and received the first year of twelve booklets, one for each month. As I read them, I could relate them directly to all the scriptures that I had read over the years, but they were the words I needed for living them now. They were the words to live them and bring them to bear on life here and now, in this physical world, in a practical and experiential way. It was a way that guided me with tools to check out for myself what God had designed for me and how I would find direction and purpose to live fully.

I wanted to experience and know the word of God, not just read and believe that life existed somewhere within It. The written words may have been there, but my experience had not given me a grasp of it at that time. With these monthly booklets

I had a renewed look with a partnership with God. The personal connection within their content became a restored reality. They became a guided companionship with the God with me. I keep reading them and find that there is always more to receive. They don't ever really read the same, as they indeed continue to awaken me each next time that I read them. The movement of Spirit greets me as I open to it. They gave me tools of courage, strength and greater awareness of my restored and sincere relationship within. They enabled me to refurbished my knowing of God with an expansion that I had been unaware. I got to practice with others, a personal ongoing transformation of experience and at the same time a lift and release into the loving presence within. The fear that was released was more precious than words, and I found the inner place with God that delivered a Self-forgiveness and restoration with my Oneness with God.

The more I participated, the more experience I was having with Emily. This was particularly true while I was on weekend retreats. They happened once or twice a year. The organization, I learned, was a formation of an ecumenical church of worldwide renown called the Movement of Spiritual Inner Awareness (MSIA). There were no church buildings, as I had known church to be. All meetings were held in homes to find what the church within each of us is, that place within where we truly gather with the Christ, as Jesus taught. He gave us the teaching, "That which I do you too shall do, and even greater things." (see John 14:12) I continue to hear and listen to this quote to this day to open myself to greater clarity and potential. Here I was finding understanding. Here I was finding the experience of being and walking with Jesus, the Christed One, who said that I too shall walk with the Presence of God as it is Christed unto me, just as Jesus once walked here to show us the Way.

John-Roger became the Wayshower for my walk and spiritual awakening to this experience here and now. The mystery of it and the awe that I felt at finding such a resource and meeting such a personhood as John-Roger led me to want to know more of who he was and how he had come to hold this focus on the planet at this time. I was to come to know myself first as a Soul, and then, with this personhood of myself, I could use all my life as a means of learning and knowing what I came here for.

I heard the lesson for me. I knew what it was. As painful as it was, I did know. I was to "Let go and let God." I had actually had those words from the scriptures on my refrigerator for years. I had realized that there was a Greater Source that I wanted to explore even when I was young. This new significance of "Let go and let God" was too bold for my heart and mind, but time would guide me in ways that only a source that I call upon as God could reveal.

The dream journeys and visions, I learned, were from my night travel inward in my Soul's Presence with God. This active movement of spirit of God was referred to as the Traveler, from the scripture I knew that talked of the Holy Spirit of God and how it shows up as a thief in the night or when not expected. It was divinely directed for my Soul's rejuvenation and awakening. Just as I traveled in the night and found revelations of life on the other side, known as visitations into the heavens and other levels of realms of spirit, so did Emily and I have visits that showed up. At first, it was simply great to see, hear, or convene with her. Some occasions were just glimpses or a knowing or feeling of her presence without actually seeing her. They were times of joyful observation and connection. They were visions of reassurance, and she at one time referred me to a spiritual teacher who was working with her, whom I saw as one of the ministers in MSIA. She was learning that she was expanding in her consciousness as I was. At other times she seemed to awaken me to something that was for my healing awareness or something I was to let go of.

One such pattern was most repetitious for years! I would find us in a series of rooms as Emily and I experienced them, with her toys and various things that she played with as well as familiar and favorite clothing. They were in color, and the spaces from room to room were often repeated and familiar from a former dream state. I'd be aware that I was in our home searching for her. In these visits, I was indeed emotionally alarmed that I had not taken care of her for some period of time now and needed to find her and resume her care to let her know that I had not forgotten her! There was a conscious anxiety and judgment on myself. How could I possibly forget to care for my daughter?

I seemed to be working this out in a repetitious manner, searching for her in my nighttime travels and dreaming. Sometimes the home atmosphere would change, but the theme was the same. Where was she? How could I, her mother, have lost contact with her? Guilt was the theme, and I played it out in these room-to-room settings that were familiar to me. I reentered them repeatedly in my search for recovery of my child. How could I possibly be so remiss of my duty? How could she be surviving without me? In desperation I would find her, I would attend to her with a loving apologetic intensity, and she would respond with a simplicity of her peacefulness and be whisked away. I would awaken, often exhausted, and wonder yet again about my job as a parent for Emily. The dream recurred intermittently over the years.

After a few years, one morning as I went into my inner spiritual time with God, I received a visitation from her. I heard her voice say to me, "I'm real. I'm real. I'm real!" and as she spoke with each statement of loving, I felt a kiss on my right cheek. It was a physically palpable touch to my cheek. I awakened to reach out for the true reality of it and found the place just at the edge of what I would sense is my aura on my right cheek. It was about eight to ten inches from my face. This was where the tactile sensation had reached into my awareness. It was a precious gift. I lay there and reveled in the peaceful assurance from her.

But it didn't stop my searching dreams throughout the years. They did become fewer, but as the years passed they would still surface for another look. By this time my spiritual awareness had been so reinforced with trust and what I thought was true acceptance of Emily and her chosen time for departure that I wondered what they were still appearing for. What was I missing in my awareness? My practice of forgiveness and all the past guilt I had rendered had moved and lifted to a great magnitude of gratitude for the eternal knowing of her life. How was this theme not finding conclusion?

So here I am, one more time searching with feelings of guilt and abandonment with perseverance to find and connect with my missing daughter; another visitation where, she again appears. This time she very clearly and sincerely with the most profound and healing completion for me with this issue. She boldly and joyfully says to me, "Mom! You don't need to look for me. I always know where you are! I know how to find you. Always, I know right where you are!"

Oh, my dear God! What a revelation. Of course! Emily is with the eternal presence of awareness of all wisdom and seeing. I am the one here with this body of restriction. But not her—she sees, and she knows. How silly of me to carry on with this need to find someone who is not lost. She is now the knower of where I am as I am of her. I don't need to keep searching for her. She is on track with me just as I have been with her throughout these years. We are not lost to each other! We are both of the eternal existence of our living love. There is so much depth and a magnitude of multidimensional factors that we are not consciously privy to, and she has shown up one more time to let me know of this eternal living. How sweet and precious to know that she looks in on me!

CHAPTER 10

Joy to Grieving—Grieving to Joy

Joy was the word that I focused on as I rose above my grieving. From the gift of joy that she brought to me in so many ways, I chose and became determined not to destroy that gift from her. I wanted to find the place in me that could hold that spark of her life that was of her essence and our existence together. It was a focus of determination to hold on to a piece of her that was intangible, but a pure essence of her being. It was something that nothing and no one could take from me, as I claimed it from a knowing and experiencing from within me. Joy is what we created and promoted in our life, and I had to have that great aspect of her with me. It was her expression of loving life that I held dear to my heart. It became the candle that lit my way as I allowed her Soul to have its journey of eternal life. It set the stage for creating my desire to go on living as the words in the song "Because He Lives" conveyed to me.

Her Soul had already chosen to go, and now it was my journey to learn to let go and find my place of survival. That was where my grieving took me. It took me into my letting her go at a time that parents are still caring and guiding and raising their children. Parenting was my absolute favorite job, and my parenting job description had taken a major reversal. She was still a child, not an adult child who had already moved on her way. Not to say that losing a child at any age makes the loss and pain any different— only that I still faced my journey of raising her, and she was no longer there. Physically, my arms tingled and ached for a long time with wanting to reach out to touch and hold her. My mind and emotions spilled out for her, and people around me were sensitive to my tears and would tiptoe around me.

I felt it. My favorite subject, my daughter, became a word that nobody would mention because I might cry. Even my family! It was as if she had never been there, and it made me feel weird. *Maybe this is just a dream, and I will wake up soon.* There was this huge disconnection from my world as I knew it. The numbing sensation that I experienced felt as though I had lost some sort of consciousness and perhaps it wasn't real. I would ask inside, *Was she really here?* It frightened me with a fear I hadn't known before. Had she just disappeared?

There was one more healing of my heart I wanted to include others in. I asked my family and close friends, "Why aren't you mentioning Emily?" It was as if my daughter, their niece, granddaughter, and friend, had been banished with a vengeance. It was choking me, and I would catch myself barely breathing. Their answer was that they worried they would make me cry; it would bring up tears and make more pain for me. So I let them know that it didn't matter; I cried anyway, and it would be nice and even helpful not to cry alone.

I asked, "Am I the only sad one here?" Then I added that if they would care to join me, it would be really wonderful. I hated crying alone all the time. Then I offered what would be helpful. "Please say what you may be thinking. Please mention her," I said. "Say it when you think of her, or say what Em would say right now if she were here or what she might do. We might even laugh with joy, sharing a memory still with us." I needed to have them include her in our gatherings as always. There was a sigh of relief, and we had a few tears together. They understood, and we all engaged in including Em in our family gatherings. It was a great help! It confirmed her existence and her eternal presence. It was another example of her ongoing presence of love with all of us and our ongoing love for her, whether she was with us or not. It defined the omnipresence of our loving as we experienced it and knew it. It brought her present for all of us.

That first Christmas my niece and nephew picked out pretty hankies for me. I told them that I always felt better after I cried, so with this precious gift they let me know it was okay. There were times when I would stop at their house just to be held by my brother-in-law and sister while I cried before going home to be alone. Their hugs and kisses were my healing helpers.

My Christmas decoration for that year was simply an ornament that I kept on display. It was an angelic child balancing on a rainbow with a bright star at the top end. It was from my sister Pamela, her husband, and the two children. To this day the children always hug generously, no matter what age they have attained or what company we are in. The children, now adults with their own children, have always been forthcoming with their hugs. Now the hugs have been multiplied with the arms of the ten children who have followed.

Thank you for them. They are more precious than words. Thank you for all the ways that God's love has been manifested with my family and through this teacher of mine and the eternal member of our family, Emily Janel.

Sometime later I was invited to a support group called Compassionate Friends. It was a local group internationally organized for parents who have lost a child. It was a place to gather monthly and talk about our children. Additionally, I could attend and share the memories and my process of getting through the days, weeks, months, and holidays. I participated for several years and after a couple of years became the facilitator for the next few years. It was a monthly opportunity, with a mutual community of parents and family, to discuss our children in a safe place where others needed to do the same. They served as functional reality checks with others who needed the same support and validation. It gave us a place to say and explore whatever we were experiencing and to check in with others who had moved ahead with the grieving process. We were in essence escorts on the way to recovery from our grief and loss. In the process we introduced our children, brought pictures, and talked about them to the others who came. It gave us a time to validate the beauty and the joy that we had experienced with our children before they passed and to cherish their lives.

CHAPTER 11

My Reflection of Wisdom

It has been thirty years now. My sweet husband, who joined my journey and made our spiritual study all possible, died, and while I was caring for him in his time of crossover, my mother also passed over. By then, at the time of their deaths, I could rejoice, knowing how connected they and I are. I knew that their physical pain was laced with joy during the time they relinquished their bodies. I didn't look for them through God as a target of proof for their existence. I knew and know the Truth that is—the Truth as witness of God's spirit of movement in me, through me, and surrounding me, with the Grace of the Eternal voice and Light of Loving.

Emily was and remains a marvelous teacher for me and my lessons for releasing, the greatest addiction to hold on rather than letting go and trusting the Grace that is the perfection of God's Being within. These are just my words to speak as best comes to me; they are feeble and will always fall short of the totality of all that is beyond our knowing. But I do know of my growth and the newness of seeing through a Higher Presence of Light and knowing there is always more. So I'll share one more piece.

A Postscript

PS: My latest awareness came recently from a spiritual counseling session to seek assistance for writing and completing this story. I had been feeling resistance to actually sitting down to reengage myself with my writing from beginning to end and figuring out what I would need to do next. My heart was asking for help and guidance. I needed the courage and energy to sit with it again.

The help came through a beloved minister and friend who does spiritual counseling and brings forward past lifetimes, clearing any pieces that may be holding us up in this lifetime. During this counsel, she assisted me in seeing my other lifetimes with Emily. What a grand awareness! I had learned and become aware of many lifetimes through the awareness of our eternal presence, but it had not even occurred to me to apply the same with Emily. How many times had we been together? My loving friend guided me through four other lifetimes when it had been my privilege to be with Emily and what those circumstances were that also led to the very short period with this lifetime. It was expansive and much more fulfilling than the short image I was holding.

This time there were actually just a few things we needed to complete together and I am the one left to joyfully know and express what that process was about for her and me. We did it. I had offered to be here for her with a sacred contract that we completed 100 percent. My heart is indeed lifted once again in one more way, with a magnitude I could not have known to even ask for many years ago, when Emily departed. But it was, indeed, the time when we began to step into this portion of our journey together.

I saw that our former lives together had already been several journeys and how full the others were. This time my challenge was to see clearly that this journey was perfect just as it was. I am even surprised with the joy of it, and I smile at the apparent comedy of it. There is comedy in having already been together so many times with wonderful lives, and this time was just one more adventure. I can laugh with the greater wisdom of it and how wonderful it has been to be together. My heart smiles unceasingly with the bigger picture and purpose. But then, that is what she came to bring me, a greater picture and the joy of life as we knew it, one more time. I am open to receive of it in the abundance that has come and will forever be. My joyful tears remind me, this love that grows deeply is exactly as I asked for and received.

Signed,
Judith Marie, Mom to Emily Janel in this lifetime

Dear God,

I begged you on the way to that emergency room that night …
Please, God, don't make me go through this experience.
Not Emi Jan, my joy and inspiration for life.
I already care for Your Children and their
Parents who must say good-bye so early.
Please don't ask me to bear that pain in order to care for others.
I do care, God. You already have my life to show Your Love.
Why do I feel so punished?
It hurts so much that I wail out in desperation for her presence.
Dear God,
Help me to know her in the Spirit of Your Presence in me.
Give me faith, and have mercy on me to know You still care and
     Love me.
I know she is now with You, she knows that Joy and Love
beyond what she could find here.
I realize how she could choose to be with You
because she loved happiness so much while she was here.
I taught her, God, that when we were not together and she was
     afraid, she was never alone … that You were always with her.
When she was violated at camp, Lord, You received her into Your
     Great Light and Love.
I know her Papa greeted her and that she dances before Your banquet.
The banquet she so cheerfully shared at camp earlier that summer.
To know that Emily has entered into that Presence of Eternal Life—
that she knows all and understands all—is overwhelming to
     my thoughts.
In the returning desperation of my loneliness,
I reach for the only comfort I can find:
Your promise that You have gone before us and have prepared
     a place,
That where You are, we may be, Emily is, also.
In God I rest with my beloved Emily Janel.

On earth I search and find God in the people who remain here
  with me,
Who tell me they love me as Emily always did, as we told each
  other every night.
"I love you, Mommy."
"I love you too, Emily."
"I love you three, Mom."
"I love you four … ever, Emily."
Emily's death does not end her life.
I endeavor to honor her life as I always have with the spirit of Joy
That always came when we were together.
Emily was always able to make it that way, wherever she went or
  whoever was with her.
That was her gift; to always let you know you were worthwhile
  and enjoyable,
Just as she came to know that of herself.
Her life made me aware of that goodness in me, so that her life
  could grow.
I struggle with the dead feelings inside of me to continue to grow and
Live for myself now:
To find new loves and be worthy so that Emily may always
Know that my love with her will never die.
As I move through my grief and
Bounce with the waves of pain, anger, and despair,
I want also to exist with her love eternally just as I want
God's love to exist through me as it always has with the gift of
  her life.

Baruch Bashan

PART THREE

LIVING WITH EMILY

CHAPTER 12

Giver of Joy

Fourth Grade School Photo

I would like to share the privilege it was for me to know Emily; to share some of the joys of our life together.

We began storybook time at three months with the hard-paged, bright colored pictures of simple words that talked of life and this reading way to learn about it. Her little chubby hands would pat the pages, animated by her excitement with the colors and the pictures. Her daddy and I would revel with her in these times of sharing and entertainment. We read often. Our day most always ended with storybook time. We delighted that as the years went by, her library of books grew and grew.

She began toddler classes when she was two where we attended Mommy and Me preschool with other toddlers and moms. As we gathered for the first time, we watched eagerly as the teacher engaged the children and communicated her enthusiasm for the importance of parenting at this early age. Emily cherished the play activities, and at this first introductory event, the teacher distributed some scarves among the toddlers and began to move with music. With full arm and body motions and inviting music, she engaged their interest. Some of the kids just weren't interested, but Emily continued after all the other children had turned their attention elsewhere. She just kept her little legs and arms in motion, with flowing scarf waving, a joyful reflection with her newfound teacher.

Emily loved the dance, and we were guided to nurture this interest in her. When she was four, she began ballet with a friend and learned all the French words for positions and moves. She continued her ballet and other types of freeform dance up until she passed.

At this same time, when Emily was four, I became a single parent. The marriage with her father had been a struggle and was tenuous at best. I thought it was going to be perfect and loving, as I trusted God for our sacred communion. But my husband put his efforts into expanding his education endeavors with multiple incompletions from one program to another. While parenting full time, working part time, it became obvious that we had come to be on different paths. He left us often for days at a time as he was supposedly studying for the ministry at his divinity program. Finally, with his third master's study curriculum, he decided to quit school. He planned to go into the pizza business, based on my financial signature since I was the one with a career. A year of counseling from our church led me to see that our marriage was no longer under God's Love and communion. So for the sake of our family and the missing ingredient of our loving for each other, I asked for a divorce. It had become obvious that a great distance had grown between us. My husband had been away so much that I felt well prepared to handle life without him. He must have wanted it that way. I was simply the one who put it on paper. (How interesting to say, I was simply the one who put it on paper).

The precious part, of course, was that Emily had been brought forth through our union. It was truly and still is the most precious experience of my life. It was a gift that I can claim as a miraculous way that God showed up for me. The memorable experience of bringing her here was a fun and interesting part of the story.

Initially our efforts to conceive were not successful. So we sought help. We went through the usual rigors: lab work to find out our potential, daily thermometer readings for ovulation, and planned insemination. It got to be tedious and not really the fun it could have been, but we continued with the doctor's recommendation, including a laparoscopy and a D and C surgical procedure.

We found that I hardly ever ovulated. But the stimulation of the scraping of the uterus did in fact release an ovum, and voilà, I was pregnant the following month. We were happy and excited and looked forward to the birth. We lived in California at the time, and I had learned of the natural childbirth technique. It piqued my interest and I definitely wanted to further investigate this opportunity. After all, I was a nurse, it involved the daddy being present, and it sounded good to me to have this experience together.

The daddy-to-be, however, came up with all sorts of resistance.

I persevered to encourage our investigation. So we headed to the introductory class with his chatter the entire way to the hospital. Through the parking lot, into the hospital entry, and up the elevator he persisted with his verbiage of doubts and reasons why. I persisted with the importance to check it out. Mid sentence, the elevator doors opened right into the classroom, and he suddenly quieted as we stood in the midst of the entire gathering.

The best thing we heard from the instructor that day was that approaching this task of delivery was comparable to preparing for an Olympic event. She said that together we could do it without numbing drugs and with healthy preparation for our child and for my body. She then added that since men were essential for the initiation of this creation, it was good and amazingly helpful to have the dads trained as well. They would be coaches for the women whom they had chosen to bring this child forward.

By the end of the class, we were all on the floor simulating contractions and practicing breathing to bypass the pain to allow the baby's loving and graceful entry to life. We were then given the opportunity to read the experiences and evaluations of those who had done this before us and see how different and also incredible each couple's experience had been.

Suddenly, Daddy-to-be was totally engaged as the perfectionist student that he always was. And this was to be almost the only task that we actually participated in together. (Well, that and the conception, I suppose.) It is one I am eternally grateful for.

Several months later, we brought forth a beautiful daughter: eight pounds, nine ounces, with lovely dark hair and eyes that immediately began exploring where she was. There was no crying, just looking and turning her head, following our voices as we spoke to her. She did get the upside-down pat on her bottom to have a little cry that the doctor said was to assure that her lungs were clear. But after a brief squeal, she promptly began gazing again, followed by some initial nursing to see what she would do with sucking. She caught on quickly, and we were on our way, with just a few bumps in the road during hospitalization and some help in the process from Lamaze classes for nursing.

As Emily began preschool, I also began some parenting education and some further professional study. I was invited to start an infant-toddler development center at our church, so I took classes toward a degree in human growth and development. I did this in preparation for the center and also to create a thesis for a master's degree. So we attended school together, Emily and I, and sometimes we were in school separately with support from friends and her parenting time with her daddy.

Her response to Daddy being away was also an indicator of the way more of the Loving showed up. While my husband and I had been trying to keep our marriage together, Emily had been grinding her teeth nightly. But within days of our separation, this behavior ceased. Then, while watching her favorite *Sesame Street* program with her thumb in her mouth, from her comfy beanbag she announced to me, "Mommy, isn't it 'elaxing'?"

It was reassuring to me that this process of marriage and what to do with the apparent commitment of it had more to do with "as long as we both shall Love" rather than "until death do us part." My commitment with God was to bring the image of Loving, which I knew was on purpose, thanks to God's gift of the Christ; to know and teach that to my child as my gratitude for the gift she was.

We continued with our daytime at the childcare center with our developed extended family there. Emily alternated weekends with her daddy. My work as a nurse supported us financially, and Emily seemed to be adjusting well.

One day the song "Just the Two of Us" was playing on the radio in the car. "Mommy, that's our song, just the two of us," Emily observed. She was right. I have to admit that we were great partners, and to this day I also have to say that she was and is my favorite and the most fun person to have lived with. That isn't to say that I am not grateful for the wonderful people and marriages that have come since. It's just that this little being was the bringer of the lessons that have, to now, produced the gift of knowing God as deeply as I can claim. My experience with her brought me to awareness of that inner Presence of my Soul that knows the connections with her soul and all those gone on before me.

As I mentioned, Emi and her daddy spent regular time together. Whatever they would do, she would inevitably find a way to include me in the experience, as if she knew that she was our connection, and she did not want me to be left out. Upon her return home from a daddy outing, she would regale me with the full story of their activities. Sometimes she even wanted to take me where she and Daddy had been, just to be sure I knew what it was like.

At an early age, Emily had definite ideas of her concept of God, and she shared them with me. One day she let me know that she had "figured it out about God." We were driving home from her Sunday school classes where she loved hearing all the stories from the Bible. In these stories, the children heard many different words that were used to refer to God. I asked her what she had figured out, and she said, "Well, I think that God is for the daddies, because He is so Big. The Lord is for the mommies because he loves them so. But Jesus is for the children, because he holds them on his lap." That worked for me! As a young child I had heard the many ways of referring to God and wondered how to relate to them, and this explanation sounded as good as any. It taught me how important it was to her to know God and how she could put Him into her life even at this early age.

All along the way, Emily was my partner and teacher. She eagerly and bravely assisted my process in creating the Infant-Toddler Child Development Center program. She even worked with me on creating curriculum for my program at the care center.

One day, as we were walking through a department store she suddenly pulled away from me and grabbed an item to show me.

"Mommy!" she exclaimed. "This would be a great 'sperience for the childrens." She proudly held up a colored, scented soap ball that would be perfect for multisensory stimulation. She knew the curriculum and how to help with it. She lived it and was proud to be the teacher with me.

Years passed while Emily and I continued on with the Child Development Center. She went through kindergarten and then first grade in our Arcadia, California, neighborhood schools. I was grateful for the multi-cultural neighborhood and classroom as well as the program for blind children where Emily experienced assisting a classmate from this program. She engaged weekly with a close friend at dance classes as we continued our relationships with all of the families that gathered at the preschool. They became our extended family, and we cared for each other's children as need arose. We had parties for the kids for their birthdays and gatherings for other happy events. It was a very nurturing time for Emily and me as we continued the transition from my marriage and the separation from her daddy.

When Emily turned seven and was about to enter 2nd grade, my father, who lived in Michigan, contracted cancer and died within that year. Not long after Dad passed, they found a cancerous tumor in my mom. It was removed, and she requested my assistance through her recovery. So Emily and I moved back to Michigan to be with my mother and my eleven-year-old sister, Beth. We moved in with Mom and Beth, and for a year Mom went through chemotherapy. She did it with ease, and she actually reversed the disease with the assistance of the holistic support program at our medical center and lots of supportive supplementation and diet adjustments that we were discovering at that time.

A year later, with the cancer gone from her body, we learned that she had moved through and released the fastest and most aggressive kind of intrauterine cancer known. She had done her work diligently, mentally, emotionally, physically, and spiritually, and she conquered the disease. Her intention had been clear.

She was the mother of an eleven-year-old who had just lost her father, and it was clear that she would stay. She told me so in a conversation when she was moving through this process.

Ten years later, Dr. Bernie Siegel came to town talking about the power of loving to reverse disease and cancer, and we were there to celebrate how Mom had achieved just that. We had come into that same awareness, and Mom, being the survivor, had embraced it. She remained with us until 86 years of age. She was such a trouper. Even with dementia and ultimately Alzheimer's at the end of her life, she held on with loving through every frustration along the way. (She was and is another great teacher for me as I move into my years of aging.)

Meanwhile, mom received the blessing of Emily's presence and loved being "Nanny" to her first grandchild. Mom was a great companion, reading books with Emily, of course, but more than that, they played games! Games were not my favorite activity, even though I knew how beneficial they could be in a child's development. But Nanny and Emily played games and games and more games! Laughter and victory whoops could be heard all through the house. And Nanny was always ready for the next round. So when I worked at the nearby Christian psychiatric hospital, I knew what the agenda would be, and I knew I would receive a full report when I got home.

Meanwhile Emily attended her new school and again began dancing. In Michigan, she joined one of her classmates at the local ballet company. Not only did she dance as she approached preadolescence, but she grew! Her legs got longer, and she was quickly approaching my height of five foot three. I knew it was inevitable that she would soon pass me by.

Her friend's mother or father usually drove the girls to dance class after school, but occasionally I was able to go. Though parents were not allowed in the room during the class, one day I peeked in to see what they were doing. The class was held in an old warehouse that had been converted into a dance studio, and the room was huge. As I opened the door, the girls were doing beautiful leaps. I watched to see if I could find Emily. Almost immediately, a pair of beautiful long legs caught my eye. The girl was making amazing leaps from one end of the cavernous room to the other. To my amazement I realized that it was Emily! The beauty of her movements took my breath away. I had seen her practice in our home, but one preparation and leap took her the entire length of our hallway. I was completely unprepared for the grace I was seeing with Emily performing leap after leap. I hold dearly in my memory the vision of her leaping. I feel blessed that I got to see the Light of God's Loving in the joy of her expression of dance. Her performance that day continues to inspire me.

Less than a year later, her dancing companion, good friend, and classmate came down with scarlet fever. Emily, being as close as she was with her on a regular basis, also came down with symptoms, and we could not relieve them, so we went to see a pediatrician. I had just been hired at the pediatric unit at Borgess Medical Center as the child life specialist and was happy to get her some special attention.

During the examination, however, I overheard the young doctor in the next cubicle say that my daughter was being overly attended to and that her mom was unnecessarily obsessed with her illness. He seemed to be taking his time to get Emily admitted to the pediatric unit despite my reporting her lack of fluid intake and the history of her exposure to her friend.

As the admissions process wore on and on, she coded. That is to say, she quit breathing and turned gray and bluish. It occurred just as a nurse walked in, and she quickly called for help. The emergency code was called throughout the hospital, and a team with resuscitative equipment arrived in the room within minutes.

In the midst of all the commotion, Emily spontaneously recovered and began breathing. But the equipment had been connected to her and showed she had had a very significant respiratory event. Then the diagnosis was confirmed: Emily had a full-blown case of scarlet fever. It was rare to see it in those days. The crucial treatment was to administer antibiotics as soon as possible. But because of the doctor's skepticism and delay that hadn't happened, and she coded. Yes, I had been extremely concerned but apparently with good reason.

Two and a half years later, while at soccer camp, referring to that incident, she told her friends about how she had died once. The following day she fell over and could not be resuscitated. Despite the timely and proper efforts of the camp staff and then the hospital personnel, nothing could be done. Emily had vacated her body.

When I consider what it was like for her, I can only recount the many times that we talked about heaven and the beautiful Light of God. Although a part of me knew she had found it and that I had done my job to prepare her as best I could, that wasn't enough for me then.

What did I miss? What hadn't I done for her? What clues had God given me that this was going to happen? My daughter was going to leave; had I been informed?

I tried to trace the recent past. It was summer, and before she left for camp, I had to work all day. Emily had a sitter and participated in some activities near our home. But she was bored and spent some time reading, drawing, and coloring for long periods. I knew she had slept some in the afternoon, which was unlike her, but she would then stay up late with me to play games and just be with me. Once I was home, we did not want to separate even for sleep.

One of the drawings she did that summer was particularly memorable. She had spent the day drawing rainbows (her favorite subject), and in the center of each one was a heart that said, "I love you, Mom." The entire sheet was covered in vivid colored rainbows and love hearts. It was beautiful and had obviously taken a great deal of time and attention. She also finished coloring a picture of a blue prize ribbon that said "#1 Mom." I had found it posted on the dresser in my bedroom.

At one point she had announced that we were remiss in not putting a rainbow decal on the back window of our new car. We had one on our old car, and she wanted it replicated. She proceeded to add one to her bedroom window as well, when we found rainbows that were suitable for her purpose.

That summer it became apparent that Emily was developing physically, and I watched my preteen turning into a young woman. She had begun her development into puberty, had her first couple of menstrual periods, and started wearing a bra. All of this change indicated hormonal shifting and entailed a new strength of emotions.

Of course, it wasn't all fun. My sweet partner Emily, who was always my negotiator and great helper, let me know in uncertain terms that adolescence was approaching when she responded one day that, no! she wasn't going to do something I had asked of her. At first I really didn't know who had spoken to me, but as the statement was repeated, I recognized my growing, strong, preadolescent daughter.

Another meaningful event had occurred while we were in church a couple of weeks prior to her going to camp. It was the Sunday of the month that the sacrament of Holy Communion was delivered to the congregation by the pastor. Emily was seated next to me as the preparation was occurring, and she turned to me, full in her awareness of what was happening, and looked up at me. She had already taken the classes covering acceptance of Christ to eventually be received into membership for communion. With tearful and loving eyes, she said, "Mom, you know how much I love Jesus. I want to have the remembrance with you." Her sincerity was so full, and as the plate was passed and the words were spoken to receive of the body and blood of Christ, I turned to her and split my serving with her and repeated the words of the minister to her to receive to herself the remembrance of Christ.

Two weeks later she went to soccer camp with her friends, where she rose into the Presence of her friend Jesus.

It was weeks later that I was led to that site on the beautiful field dug out from the hillside by the waters where she fell over and left her body. I asked to sit in the place where her soul had chosen to move on. I wanted some quiet and private time to sit at this site that was sacred to me. I held on to my Bible and thanked God for all the scriptures that I knew of then and would come to know more fully as the life of this child continued to teach me. We are surely and truly all teachers to each other and Emily was and is mine. The blessing continues.

Did she know what was coming? Had she seen? Where was my comfort in this? How do I listen to this evidence and determine whether I should have known what was to come? *Please, God, let me know* became my fervent prayer after losing Emily.

CHAPTER 13

Emily and Pets to Veterinarian

Emily loved having her pets. They gathered early in her life while she attended our Presbyterian preschool in California. They were small animals and were used to teach the children about caring for life and having thoughtful consideration.

It all started on her fourth Christmas when the pet rat in her preschool classroom delivered the multiple gifts of new babies. They all needed homes, and Emily was among the eager homemakers. She began her negotiations for bringing home a pet rat, and we learned how to care for and make a home for this rodent, now to become a pet. He was black and white, and after the many hands that held him at the preschool center, he was tamed and really very responsive to the attention given by the children.

He was named Templeton, after the noble rat in *Charlotte's Web*. We had read the book and watched the movie several times each. Templeton lived in his cage on the bookshelf in her bedroom, and of course, being nocturnal, he exercised on his wheel most of the night, which never seemed to interrupt her deep sleep. But Emily was good at attending to him, giving him exercise time out of his cage, feeding him with assistance, and learning his needs.

The next pet was a bunny rabbit delivered at Easter. Emily named her Sanne Sweetheart from her very own imagination. Sanne (long *e*) grew and hopped around with Emily in and out of its elevated outdoor cage in the enclosed backyard. She liked feeding Sanne from scraps at the table, and despite occasional scratches, she handled, held, and hopped with her new bunny friend. Again, she thought it would be a "good 'sperience for the childrens." So Sanne came to visit at the child development center and was totally comfortable hopping around inside and outside with the "childrens." The children adored the visits and learned to respect this little form of life.

This was when Emily's father and I went through a separation and divorce. Also, my mother became a single parent with eleven-year-old Beth after the death of my father. When Mom was diagnosed with cancer, we returned home to live with her and Beth and support her through her therapy.

Emily was seven years old when we prepared to move from California to Michigan. It was a hot summer day, and Templeton was brought outside as we cleaned and packed. As we busied, the sun moved into his territory, and I'm sorry to say he was temporarily forgotten. As a result, Emily and I had the first experience for her with the death of a pet. But prior to this a fluffy gray kitten also arrived to live with us whom she called Puffer. Puffer was a boy, but Emily didn't want it to be a boy, so we just referred to "her" and we proceeded to Michigan with the two remaining pets. Puffer lived primarily in the basement quarters Emily and I shared, where we lived with my mom (Nanny to Emily) and Beth. But within the year, Puffer ended up with some prostate problems. We had actually forgotten "she" was a male, and Sanne Sweetheart who lived outside and needed extra attention during the winter didn't get it. It was a very emotional and sad time for Emily with the passing of all three of her pets that year. There were tears and "but Mommy" as we talked about life and caring about pets and what happens when they are not well attended to. Among all the transition and weather changes, we had neglected the pets and their needs.

The next pet that came was more of a family project between the four of us. It was a sweet yellow tiger who moved in and was quickly named Tigger, after the Winnie-the-Pooh character. Emily soon proclaimed ownership. The tough-love part came when our departure to our own condo meant leaving the little golden tiger where it knew its home and where my sister and Mom had also attached to his presence.

Emily nestled in tree with Penelope Ann (Penny)

So we made and committed to a plan for Emily to assist in the earning and purchasing of her next pet. We researched and chose to find just the right kind of dog. We spent library and reading time to find the right breed to invite into our home, a home-bred dog with the temperament that would be healthy and loving. She worked her chores and took responsibility and saved her earned money to pay for half of the expense. We eagerly took time to read the pet ads from the local papers to find the right cocker from a forthcoming litter. We made contacts and visited a family who would soon have the delivery. We visited again after the puppies were born to make our choice and waited for them to grow and be ready to come to their new homes.

GOOD FRIENDS! Emily and Alicia in tree between our homes.

The buff cocker we chose looked every bit the color of a one-cent coin, and we named her Penelope Ann to be called Penny. Training Penny became Emily's 4-H project. She learned how to train and be the master guide of her dog, which was really quite amazing to watch. She started on her own with books from the library and a training leash to practice what she read. She became totally frustrated when all Penny would do was roll over and pee on herself as she called the commands! What was wrong with her dog? What would she do? She was sure she was doing what it said. She needed help from someone.

First dog training photos of Emily, Penny and 4H Instructor

So we approached the 4-H opportunity with fear and questions. Was this dog actually capable? Was Penny demented in some way? We arrived at the farm where the other peers and dogs were assembled in a ring, and Emily was invited in to have Penny sit and then give her the command to heel as she tugged on the leash. Emily had already tried this command but followed the guidance into the ring where all the other dogs were doing just that and to our great surprise, voilà! Penny did as the other dogs were doing! She sat as commanded. She walked next to Emily and heeled! Whew. Penny was smart after all. What fun this would be!

Emily was delighted to become the master trainer for her puppy, and they practiced diligently. Soon the 4-H group attended shows at the county fairs and occasional other dog exhibitions, and Emily and Penny came home with many prize ribbons. They were very proud companions. With Emily as the master trainer, Penny was the willing, obedient recipient.

It was a great camaraderie that was more than just a child and her dog. Emily came home daily from school before I came home from work at the hospital, and Penny was the happy cropped tail-wagging greeter. They would play, they would read, Penny would be fed, and then they would do some practice commands and routines. They even slept together: Penny with her head on her pillow, Emily with her head on her pillow. Penny snored loudly; Emily slept. There was even a third companion after a while when a black kitty was adopted from her favorite veterinarian friend. Ebony joined in for the loving and snuggled with the clan.

Life was good. The inspiration had been set. Emily talked of becoming a veterinarian. She would really like a horse like one of her friends, but the cost would take some time to deal with. After seeing the litter from which Penny had arrived and the cost for one dog, she created a plan. She would breed Penny and save for the horse and its care. It was an ongoing conversation of challenge and negotiation.

Multiple Sclerosis Readathon Winners. Emily 1ˢᵗ Prize Completion.

The following year a new challenge was given to the fifth graders at her school, called the Multiple Sclerosis Read-a-Thon. Emily had been requesting a larger two-wheel bike, and we had a dear friend, Barbara, with MS. And being the reader that she was, she knew that she was going for the first prize which was a beautiful two-wheel bike. She came home with instructions that she would need to read one book a *day* to win first prize! I was surprised at such an expectation, but Emily was not altered. She wanted to help our dear friend so she could get well, and she had a goal! I came home to find her and Penny closed in and cuddled on the bathroom floor with pillows and her book for the day. I did indeed sign her form nightly that the next book was read word by word, and she captured the first prize that not only included the bike but all the other levels of prizes that were accomplished along the way! I did learn that the directions weren't quite as she told them to me. But she chose her goals and achieved them. She was very determined that way.

I am happy to say that she had a very strong self-esteem and knew what she wanted and could plan how to proceed to get there. If it wasn't to my immediate liking in some way or another, some serious negotiating would ensue, and an amicable direction and agreement would be arranged for a win–win goal for both of us. I came to learn that I could plan on it this way. Preadolescence had begun. She was developing and began her menses, and she grew five inches that year, as I recall. She and her close friend her size had talked, and she let me know that they had decided they were never going to wear a bra.

Soccer Team. Star Goalie – Emily in black shirt.

She danced at the studio with another dear friend and played soccer every week with her community friends at school, and we went to weekly church services and gatherings. Along with that, she excelled in her studies. I was always challenged with what would satisfy her growth and development, and since I had studied years earlier for my master's in human development, I found it necessary and enjoyable to keep up with my parenting needs for her growth and enthusiasm for life. She was the eldest among her cousins, who gathered and lived nearby, and she was the creator of the play and games that they all enjoyed. The cousins loved being with her, and they all looked up to her. She cherished each of them, and they played and laughed until time to go home at the end of another day.

Last photos taken of Emily and Penny before Dog Show

The last summer she was with us, she competed at a dog show. She traveled there with the 4-H club without my attendance. She asked if she could have her hair done at a salon. Her hair was heavy and straight down to her waist, and she wanted to have a fancy braid that she had seen in a magazine. So she and her hairdresser proceeded with a design. She called me at work to say how long it had taken and that she was wearing a thick circular braid on the top of her head. She said it felt like a crown. I have a wonderful picture of her and Penny just prior to leaving showing Penny with her nose lifted up to Emily's face as the two of them were about to kiss. It is very sweet and a favorite of mine, complete with the royalty of her crown and new pants to go with her growing long legs.

This was also the summer that she went to camp for the first time. She had never wanted to go and sleep somewhere before this time, and this summer she engaged in camp with her best friend from church at our church camp on Lake Michigan and then attended soccer camp with friends from school.

Church camp was very special, and the stories that came home afterward were very rich as she shared the scriptures that were meaningful for her and talked of her camp counselor and her cabin mates. I was eager to see her and arrived to pick her up way before anyone else had arrived. Being a bit uncomfortable and not knowing where to wait, I left the area, did a short errand, and then arrived back for her late! I missed meeting all her friends, and she was incredibly disappointed.

For this lapse I felt incredibly guilty for years to follow. Our young minister, who was the chaplain at camp that session, told beautiful and exciting stories of how her peers had loved and enjoyed her and the many plays that epitomized how central she was to the events. I had missed being included with her enthusiasm, so rich with the loving of God's expression that week. I have managed to find forgiveness for myself, but now I know that it was my time to let her go into her journey there with God's guidance—not with mine nor with my agenda, but it was every bit between her and her newfound relationship with God and Jesus, her friend who would hold her on His lap. I am thankful for the knowing and my growth as she grew into her ascension.

But Penny waited for her to come home. She had been bred to have puppies before Emily left, and Emily had told her, "Now don't you have your babies before I get home!" It turned out that Penny had a false pregnancy. When Emily left for camp, Penny found a sock she had worn and held onto it as she waited for Em to come home. She had grasped onto it and kept it near her. She was, after all, the official greeter and was loyal to her task.

When I entered the house every afternoon after work, Penny would grab her sock, jump onto Emily's bed, and look at me with her tail wagging. It was an unceasing message: *Where is she? Where is my master, my best friend, Emily? I know she wouldn't leave me. I can wait and watch.* And so with unending loyalty, she did. For weeks that grew into months, she held the sock until only threads remained. Then one day, I heard this awful groaning, squealing noise come from Emily's room. I went and found Penny under her bed as if crying. She had lain with me many times in her room as I would hold Emily's pillow or pj's and just cry out for her with the fragrances of the clothing and of her room, and now Penny was having her turn. It was heart-wrenching, and I held her and prayed for her comfort as I did for my own. I was all she had, and I could never replace Emily, the one she looked for. I even went to training sessions a few times to learn her commands and bring her to a familiar setting. But as diligently as I made the effort, Emily could not be replaced.

The most important advice that I could give to families who have lost a child would be to inquire if there is a significant pet or dog who will be aware of the absence of this child. They should bring that pet to the funeral home or to the hospital where the child may be preparing to pass. I played out that scene in my mind many times wishing that I had brought Penny to the neighborhood funeral home to see where Emily's body had arrived, where she had come to rest, so Penny could somehow have closure. It was torturous to be with this loving companion of Emily and to have excluded her from the process. Bless this sweet dog and her endurance and loyalty to Emily.

However, this story with Penny does not stop here. Five years after Emily passed, I ended up selling my home to a lovely family; the husband and father was to be the new minister at a neighboring Wesleyan church. Prior to this my brother, Ted, and his wife had moved in and helped me to put Emily's room and things away. I needed something to bring me to this passage, and their loving presence made it possible. I agreed to sell the home to the husband and wife and two children, a daughter and son.

Their daughter was named Emily, and the conversation naturally turned to my daughter, which is how they became aware of Emily's passing and the support of my family. I was preparing to move to a home with some friends and entertaining a new partnership with Jim, who would become my next husband. As we talked and got acquainted, this family fell in love with Penny and her joy with the children. Then, through our negotiations they also offered to give Penny a home should I ever need or choose to do so.

In time I saw that Penny wasn't getting the attention that she needed with the schedule I was living, and after consulting with my family, we chose together to have Penny return to the home she knew to have children to play with. So I made the call—they had kept my old number for convenience—and Emily answered the phone. I greeted her, "Hello, Emily, this is Judy. I'm calling to ask if you and your family would still be interested in having Penny dog in your home. She needs children to love and play with, and I know she would like being with you."

The accumulation of synchronicities was quite something. We arranged for Emily to check with her parents. They responded affirmatively, and the next day, I brought Penny back to the home that she knew. I was given visitation rights any time I wanted to be there, and I did get back to see her quite often. There were times when my car just went back to that neighborhood after work. I needed to check out my past for a bit of remembering and to see our wonderful neighbors where one of Emily's best girlfriends, Alisha, resided next door. I sat with Penny on the front step, where Emily had sat with her last, sharing enthusiasm to see each other and gathering a few licks of kisses.

One day the pastor and family were transferred, and I was given a call to say good-bye to Penny. They told me that Penny had experienced a bout with cancer and released a tumor. They hadn't known if she would make it. They were about to contact me when she pulled through. She chose to live on and be with her new Emily and brother, and that was the last that I heard of her. By now Penny will have transitioned to the other side also. I know where her companionship is. I can see them with all their joy, a very busy tail wagging, and lots of kisses. I am happy for them. I can smile with my tears, knowing what it looks like.

Postscript

Emily had started talking about what she wanted to become and looked at careers. Top on her list was to become a veterinarian. After her passing, her daddy created a memorial fund in her name to support an adoption and rescue program for pets. Her love for animals continues.

CHAPTER 14

Becoming a Writer

I think Emily became a writer just to mimic the fun of all the words she was reading. She loved her words and her expressive vocabulary. She loved reading them on paper and in books and then she eagerly wrote them and recorded them. She read author by author just as we would choose in library outings when she was younger. In each book we read, we acknowledged the author by name and then the artist who drew the pictures and how together they had presented us with this opportunity to read this storybook.

Emily at home with Ballet pose – 5ᵗʰ Grade

Our choices and themes were varied from the days of cardboard books to Dr. Seuss and then from pets and ballet to growing-up stories of families and children in school with Judy Blume, Beverly Cleary, and many other chosen authors. Her personal library grew to more than two hundred books plus all that we enjoyed from the library. Even as we started in the library finding authors on the shelves from A to Z, so did she find the fascination of following authors she learned about in school and read all the editions.

She began writing her own stories, from an early preschool cassette-taped version, and then continued her writing through her remaining classes in school. I have some of her early first editions that began in preschool, and then by the time she was six, they became bound versions created in her first through third grade classroom. But as the tape recorder was being introduced, I also have some versions and expressions from her voice. I have never written this story but have found the tape and want to include it here. And I quote from her sweet little voice at six years old. Her voice is very slow and distinct as she speaks into the cassette player.

"The Christmas Story" by Emily Losey

One day a lit-tle [emphasis on the t's] boy was cut-ting trees and get-ting logs for the fireplace.
He lost his way in the snow. [a breath] Of course.
In the summertime he had a trail to get home. [pause]
But *now* [a bit louder] the snow covered the trail.
Luckily he had a shovel. He shoveled his way home.
He dropped the logs along the way.
When he got home his mother said, "Why are you so late?"
He told her about *that*: the shovel and the trail.
Then she said, "Where are the logs?"
He said he dropped them on his way home.

[umm] He went out—back and he found the logs.

He came back and they sat by the fireplace and drank hot cocoa with their meal.

The End.

Her third grade edition was entitled, "Purple with a Little Bit of Pink," where two elves turned colors with the problem that they had with walking and talking too much. One turned pink, the other purple. All the people laughed at them until they turned red. Help arrived for the two elves, and the whole community became normal when Santa appeared as he rode through the stars and made everyone normal with his spell of a "Merry Christmas."

It is actually very insightful as she recognized differences and then how we all can come together with acceptance for each other. As she began her writing world she enjoyed reading her stories at family gatherings for Nanny and her aunts and uncles along with the cousins.

By fifth grade she was producing pages of episodes asking me to please type them for classroom studies. It was a special event when Emily read her first fifth-grade story that year at school. This first one in the fall was entitled, "One Boring Halloween Night." She was invited to read her story to the third-grade class during the lunch period. Later that day she greeted me with excitement as I arrived home. "Mom, today I read my story to the third-grade classroom, and when I was finished, they clapped! They all *clapped* Mom!" She continued to be called upon, as did other classmates to read to the third-graders with the next editions of her stories.

That same year she was chosen, with some of her classmates, to attend the young authors workshop sponsored by one of the departments at Western Michigan University. She brought the last story that she had written that year. It is about a lost black cocker spaniel and is written in the voice of Licorice, the dog. She completed her writing career with this endearing story of this cocker who was looking for a home. She was surely inspired by her own buff-colored cocker spaniel, but this one in her story is black and actually mimicked the image of the first puppy Emily had chosen from the litter, which as it happened did not come home with us. She and I had already fallen in love with this little black one, but that one became ill and we were encouraged to choose another. I think she then brought him forward in this story to find him the home that we didn't provide.

It has many episodes in it, and again she got out the push-button tape recorder to verbalize her thoughts and ideas for getting them down on paper. She expressed frustration at not being able to remember her ideas after she said them, so I offered my handheld recorder for her to listen to her voice and process her stories. Her episodes in the story tell us that we all find help when we are simply searching for love and how it always shows up. "All I Need Is Love" is the title, and the puppy eventually finds a home. As Em had learned of God as the giver, guide, and bringer of the loving, so it is that she brought the loving to her pages for a puppy who found and received his source for Home. And now it is that Emily dwells in that place of her eternal living, at Home in the Heart of God as she knew it and professed it in her stories of finding it.

I have kept these recordings, and when I listen to them I can still hear her words and her ideas as she calls out, "Mom! Mommy, can you help me?" I am already plunking away on the typewriter, and we laugh when I say to her, "Emily, how much help can one person give?" as we make our way through the next words to be printed. I am busy clicking away on the standard push-key typewriter, getting the pages out before bedtime to complete the homework for the next day. The sound of our exchange remains stamped and sealed in my mind and heart. I smile with this joyful time of our relationship. I hear her say, "Mom, can you help me? What word am I looking for?" I listened and I offered, but her response was inevitably, "No, that's not it!" and she would find her own words that worked for her.

Emily Janel Losey Composer/Writer
"A Rainbow to Read"

All of these last written fifth-grade stories are now in the compiled edition called *A Rainbow to Read*, named by Uncle Marve, who thought it fitting after reading and compiling her artwork filled with her favorite rainbows. The stories were truly a colorful reflection of her rainbows and the life she grew into. They are in print to acknowledge the writer she had succeeded in becoming.

CHAPTER 15

Postscript: The Emily Losey Citizenship Award

Emily graduated from fifth grade at Starr Elementary School and was to enter middle school in Plainwell, Michigan, the coming fall of 1983.

Mr. Vermeulen, also known as Mr. V, was her last homeroom teacher, with whom she spent most of her time in fifth grade. She grew in her enthusiasm for learning from her other teachers at Starr, but especially from Mr. V. Daily she would come home to tell of a situation, story, or learning experience from Mr. V. He was a tall healthy man and creative with his classroom instruction and let the children know how much he enjoyed them. His respect and caring for each of them was a model for how they treated each other and Emily found a safe, stimulating, and rewarding atmosphere for learning in the classroom and with her classmates.

Along with stories of her friends, she loved telling a daily story of Mr. V and what he had done that day. One day she came home to tell me what she had figured out about Mr. V. She declared that he used the same deodorant as her dad! She giggled as she said it and turned red with embarrassment. It turned out that Mr. V was much taller than the classmates, and when standing next to him, one's face is pretty much at his armpit! I told this story at one of the award assemblies at her school after her passing. It brought the gymnasium full of students to laughter and smiles.

THE EMILY LOSEY AWARD

Twin City News Photo

Emily Losey was a 5th grade student at Starr Elementary School during the 1982-83 school year. During that year, Emily was an outstanding example of what is best about young people. Her <u>concern</u> for others was shown by earning over $300 for the M.S. Read-a-thon and by the many friends she had. Her <u>involvement</u> in activities included the annual school talent show, special chorus, ballet, AYSO soccer, 4-H and her church. Her strong desire for <u>achievement</u> allowed her to win a first place in the 5th grade science fair and have her Young Authors book selected as one of the best in her grade. Emily's warm outgoing personality made her an immensely popular girl. Tragically, Emily passed away on August 11, 1983.

The Emily Losey Citizenship Award is the highest honor a student at Starr School can earn. It was created to honor the memory of Emily Losey and to recognize one fifth grader each year who best exhibits concern for others, involvement in activitives, and the ability to successfully achieve that Emily exemplified.

Emily Losey Citizenship Award created by Mr. E. Vermeulen

It was Mr. Eric Vermeulen who created an honorary award in her memory as a model for the students at Starr Elementary School. It was a collaboration with the other teachers and principal and became a yearly event at the close of the school year: the Emily Losey Citizenship Award assembly. The students qualified for nomination by earning and receiving a monthly certificate for Citizen of the Month, by nomination of any of the teachers in recognition and even by self-nomination and the desire to write for themselves how they would qualify. He described three qualities that were exemplary of Emily as a model. It was written to encourage students to follow her example of (1) concern for others, (2) involvement in the school and community, and (3) achievement of positive goals.

It is the top citizenship award given at this final assembly of the year for the third to fifth graders. The students each write why they would be suitable for the award, and then all are recognized at the assembly. One student is chosen by a panel of teachers for the final Emily Losey Citizenship Award. This person's name is then printed on a gold plate and added to the list of previous honorees, along with Emily's picture on a plaque. This began in 1984 and continues to this day. The course of this event eventually turned to include an expansion of awards for every child to receive acknowledgement of a unique quality of learning each one represents. It's a goal of conduct for the children, and parents are invited and included to attend this final recognition before entering middle school.

It warms my heart, and I am awed at the manner in which this event is cherished. For years I attended the event and told some related story of Emily and something of her experience at Starr and then would announce and bring forward all the candidates who pursued this award. I then opened the secret envelope to read the name of the person who was the chosen winner and hand them the gold plate with their name on it for this honorary accomplishment.

Parents and students alike would ask me if it wasn't hard for me to be there. Well, yes, it usually brought up some of my emotions, but only before and after did my emotions of loss and love need caring for. But during the actual attendance with all those children, knowing that Emily was one of them at one time was always a joy and in a way let me be with Emily. It was her favorite place, and I continued to go and share the space.

Each year I was given a time to talk about her and something in relation to how much she enjoyed learning, writing, and participating at this wonderful school that they all attend. Copies of *A Rainbow to Read*, which included six of her stories, were given out to the candidates, and they would ask me to sign them. I signed them with the privilege of having been her mother. "En-Joy! From Emily's Mom" is what I wrote. Joy was the gift she had brought to me, and I wanted them to receive this portion of it as I had.

Other Honorariums

1. 4-H Emily J. Losey Award:
    A financial gift of $180.00 toward the Camp Kids Memorial for pet care and training
2. A Neighborhood Memorial to Ransom Public Library:
    Our Timber Oaks Street neighborhood where we lived gathered a remembrance of Emily
    Donation to the Plainwell community library
3. Emily Citizenship Award: From All-Starr Parent Group; Designed by Mr. E. Vermeulen
4. Camp Wakeshma Soccer Field: Renamed the Emily J. Losey Soccer Field
5. Borgess Pediatrics Memorial: Emily J. Losey $1,000.00

My Prayer

Dear Father, Mother God,
I am open to receive of the vision of this creative process.
It appears with the freedom of my expression
an exercise of my vision
my revelation of words to write.
A revealing to me of messages
from my Soul to speak and be heard,
It is for me to listen, that I might find awareness
of a memory for insight and healing.
I don't necessarily consider myself creative, but it appears
as an awareness that I might be more conscious
in my present existence as it reflects from the past.
This process comes in with my intentions of doing or don't.
I let it percolate for a while, getting heated to steaming.
Listening for incentive with the forceful hissing of
incompletions with hidden procrastination.
Fear and judgment blocking my aimless efforts.
On course for what I am to learn,
again, yes again, I forgive myself for irrational judgments.
Feelings, thoughts, bouncing around
grabbing at my mind and heart.
It's time to *Let Go* of the illusions;
misperceptions of loss and guilt
begging for attention and release.
I take a scoop of courage and acknowledge the next bit to *learn*.
Let's move on, I say to myself from a voice of encouragement.
Settle into acceptance with the helping hand of grace
highly and freely given with no strings attached!
The momentum of it pushes me into process
with integrity for purpose
holding my shriveled heartstrings with the rays of gratitude
for Loving One daughter and One man into the Heavens.

PART FOUR

LIFE WITH JAMES THORNTON DAILY

CHAPTER 16

Introduction

In the fall of 2004 on Friday, September 24, Jim and I joined all of the southern shoreline communities evacuating from Gulf Shores, Alabama, with the onslaught of Hurricane Ivan. We had left our dream life of ten years on the tenth floor of our beautiful condominium to live in a small condo down the West Beach while we worked on the design plans to build a home on our lot at the Peninsula Racquet Club. Every week we spent hours of exercise time at the club playing tennis with a great company of friends and playmates. We had purchased a lot, years before with a vision of someday departing from a crowded beach road, knowing that this would be our ideal scene.

That time had come, and six weeks after our move to the West Beach in Gulf Shores, Hurricane Ivan visited us expending a swirling fury of damaging wind and a massive downpour of rain directly overhead. We moved six more times that year and finally sold our properties and in the fall of 2005 led ourselves to higher ground in Birmingham, Alabama. We were guided to a lovely European-like traditional neighborhood development (TND) called Mt Laurel where all the trees prevailed and homes of varied sizes and plans were available, surrounded by parks, lake, walkways and comforts of nature. In spring of 2007, we experienced a drought that created a blanket of pollen on a daily basis. No one escaped the resulting upper respiratory disturbance. The results for Jim were ultimately terminal.

We had moved into our home and got acquainted with our new community, but the friendships that Jim left behind became irreplaceable. The tennis games on the new Pelham courts were not what he had become accustomed to or the desired challenge of competition.

A best buddy from his former camaraderie of friends at the Peninsula courts died which was an unspeakable loss for Jim. He wouldn't talk about it and never called him before he departed to say good-bye or express his feelings.

He was unwilling to pick up the dance lessons we had initiated before we fled from the hurricane, even though they were available right in our neighborhood.

He had paid off all his financial debts, which he announced was his life goal. Then, with his love for numbers, he focused his attention to mastery of the game of Sudoku, something that very few accomplished.

I look back to examine these times for us to see whether the course of his departure was revealed. A counseling friend suggested that I try an exercise of stretching and expanding into all of the spaces of our bed. The focus was intended to assist me with writing what could be revealed for comfort or some insight now that Jim was no longer with me. What might I learn of his journey and our end of time together for my acceptance of his passing?

So here I am. I find myself alone on a small space of our king sized bed in our newly designed bedroom in Mt Laurel. We chose a gorgeous fabric that particularly suited us, with white satin leaves and an azure and gold toned nature motif for the bed frame. We painted the bedroom walls with a matching blue and placed antiqued mirrored bedside tables to reflect the tones of color and light. The head and foot of the king-sized bed were simply cushioned, rounded, and flat, without much height, and the bed itself sits low to the floor. I had not chosen the high elevation of the current style. I chose this one for safety and a peaceful loveliness as I envisioned our elder years here in our home.

The deluxe nature of the bed is found in the natural rubber layers of the mattress that we researched for health and comfort. We traveled to Atlanta, Georgia, to check out the benefits of this natural rubber material and made our choice for this most nurturing piece of furniture for our new Craftsman style home. It was and is the most expensive purchase in the home and represented the amount of value we placed on sleep and the time we spent doing that. We loved the ease of getting in and out of this bed and the comfort of it as it sits on a frame of wooden dowels for support and weight distribution. It is truly the most deluxe preparation for sleeping through the night that I have known in this lifetime.

So now that Jim is no longer here, I consider taking a new opportunity for my time in this bed alone. I am exploring the spaces of it to see what thoughts or memories come to me. My friend said to me that this could be a way to get some clarity after going through a loss or crisis. So I went ahead and made it a point to change positions to give myself the experience of it. I asked myself, what is it like to explore the different spaces? If this bed were to represent the size and experiences of my life with Jim, then I could feasibly find some new experiences and perhaps become aware of something that I had not recognized or realized before.

Yes, right here with this platform as a stage for a period in our life, I am asking, listening, and reflecting toward what may appear. I'm looking to see if there are different levels of comfort. What can I learn about myself in relationship with Jim here in the large spaces of this bed?

When Jim was here, I just slept on my side of the bed, a distance from him especially since he stayed very much on his side of the bed. In fact, he slept not only on his side, but remained mostly to his edge of the bed. So I asked, If I moved closer to his side of the bed, could I find a closeness to him? Would it be a way to embrace him, and might some fragrance of him be released?

His process with death was fast, and the time was spent in deep compassion with attending to his needs. It was simply sweet but too fast to give me time to process all that it meant to me. Not that we hadn't talked about our time of departing from each other, because we did. But as I lay there, I was not sure that I even knew the weight that the whole experience took in my thoughts. We had so many wonderful experiences together. This one, however, was *not* meticulously planned out, as so many others were. We always talked about our activities ahead of time and carefully scheduled them, but we hadn't really said what it would be like to depart from each other at this early stage of our lives. We were sure that we would be together at least another ten or even twenty years.

We did hold an ongoing spiritual practice of departure as we slipped into sleep in the evenings. Every night through meditation, we practiced leaving our body, intending to rest in the healing arms of God's Love. We held this focus to ask for the Light of Father/Mother/God to fill, surround, and protect us as we refreshed our Souls and rested our bodies to prepare for another day through our nighttime sleep and travels. We loved the gift of our sleep in the new comfy bed and slept well in the colors and comfort of the room, right down to the peaceful quiet of the matching blackout waffle shades! Nightly, we departed our bodies with our study of Soul Transcendence for preparation of our ease of final departure someday.

We had even chosen to update our will and trust since we had made so much transition with our home dwellings this last couple of years following Hurricane Ivan. This had all been handled and nearly completed when the diagnosis of esophageal cancer came to Jim.

So, yes, we had been in preparation for … someday, way in the future, but not now! It appeared to me when the first words were spoken and the suggestion was also made on the CT scan that it could also be a hiatal hernia, I was in full agreement with the hernia, having recognized all the allergic reactions Jim had always had with foods and the heavy season of allergy and pollen from the drought we were experiencing.

This all occurred at our new residence in Birmingham in the spring of 2007. Hernia made absolute sense! That was what created all the coughing for so many years, and it was just worse during this awful allergic season. We were all coughing, me included. We even sounded identical with this respiratory cough of the season! The only difference was that I had ceased coughing after a couple of weeks. All our neighbors as well had suffered after this heavy drought with the allergic cough as the golden pollen filled the air and settled everywhere, forming its yellow blanket. It passed, and we got to the other side of it, but Jim did not. His coughing continued.

So now I lay here and reflected that when Jim was here, he only slept on his very own edge of the bed. He would get up and down during the night and climb back in onto his edge pulling the sheet as he slid off and back on again. I became aware of his process with this up and down behavior during the night for frequent urination. I never heard him, but I knew of his movements from how far the sheet was pulled toward his edge of the bed in the morning.

I don't know if he ever did claim his half of the bed or moreover came to find me where I was on my half of the bed. He simply stayed with his edge. Was he already *edging out of life* on the new bed? Was he giving off clues that he was just satisfied with what was left of his lifetime as he approached the end of his time with me?

It wasn't new for me to stretch across from my side of the bed and not be able to touch him. My arm was not long enough to reach him before I fell off to sleep. As open and rich as the bed was for our remainder of our lives, we never fully restored our companionship. Life as we had known it was changing. The signs were not clear yet as to what was happening, but reflectively we were not completely into our full loving expression here in the new home and bed. There was a large piece of him missing from when we had lived at the beach before the hurricane. I don't know if I ever really found Jim again after we moved into the new home. It was home for me, but I don't know that it was for him.

He was preparing for a different home, the One we found so often from within—the One that was the eternal dwelling that for twenty years together we had practiced for, not the one here on the bed.

CHAPTER 17

Our Time to Meet

Five years after Emily passed, in 1988, I was privileged to meet Jim (James Thornton) Daily. It was not part of my awareness but after attending the first Insight Transformational Workshop and some gatherings thereafter, others who came to know me who knew Jim let both of us know that we needed to meet. We had both attended these workshops without actually meeting until a collaborative friend coordinated our invitation for an upcoming party with some of the insight participants. After meeting and watching him throughout the evening, I did some inner consenting that led me to ask him to join me as my date at a forthcoming social event. I held two tickets to the local summer barn theater, along with eighteen others who had attended the Insight trainings with us, and I wanted to invite someone to join me. I had decided that this time, as a single female after two other marriages that were not as successful as I had hoped, I would do the asking!

But first, I had to contend with an affair that had been initiated after the second Insight training that I had just completed. One gentleman, who was also Jim's current best friend, had a deep crush on me, and with the loving essence we all depart with after a workshop such as this, I had entertained him for a couple of dates in the last couple of weeks. He was quite a bit younger than me, and although it was a nice experience to be so well thought of, I knew that this relationship would not be my preference. He also knew that I held these tickets and mentioned to Jim that he thought I would be asking him to the "Barn." So as the weekend approached I spoke with him personally to let him know my thoughts regarding our friendship and that I indeed would be asking Jim to join me for the theater event. I let him know that I was speaking to him first because I wanted to be grateful and respectful to his process with my decision.

We moved on, and I called Jim that Thursday for the Saturday night date. The Red Barn Theatre was truly a resurrected formerly functioning barn with well installed staging and lighting, gradually elevated hardwood seating, and an acoustical pit for live orchestration. The outside field was grassy, and the performers directed traffic and parking in the field before the performance.

We arrived to meet our friends and pick up our tickets to find that most of the tickets were seated together except for two that were located front and center. The set of two were placed in my hand. I smiled inwardly as I saw the setup. They would all be seated behind us, watching our first date. They were among those who had recommended that Jim and I were to meet. They had also attended with us through the healings and transformations of the Insight trainings, along with their own processes. We were all cheerleaders for each other.

Now here were Jim and I, in these two third-row center seats to see the comedy presentation, *La Cage aux Folles*. Well, a comedy it was! At one point the laughter broke out in such a way that Jim erupted with laughter! It was a deep, pervasive, gut-wrenching "Hah, hah, hah!" that was glorious to hear! The audience began to quiet down, but Jim's enjoyment of what had just transpired on stage was still in full swing! The performers kept still on stage, holding their tableau without moving into the next dialogue, as Jim finished laughing. Of course our friends, who were watching from the long row of seats not far behind us, were also enjoying the comedy and the laughter, and we were all thoroughly engaged in hearing Jim's joy and appreciation of the success of the production. It was a night to remember, and I still see it and feel it within me. It was laughter that we both needed and received as a gift for our healing with this new moment of a budding friendship.

Afterward, reservations had been made for a post-cabaret show with the performers in an adjacent shed with limited and very close seating at small tables. It was then, as we all sat close together, that Jim placed his warm hand on my back with some light touch and massage. It was a comforting, healing touch that we both hungered for and savored in those moments of song and more laughter. The night ended with an invitation for our next date a week later. We finished the evening with our first kiss as he walked me to the door. The moonlight shone just over his right shoulder as I looked up at him and received the gentle warmth of his lips.

The following date ended with an even more engaging kiss. As he embraced me and we kissed, I went into a state of timelessness and sank into a place far from any awareness of my present surroundings. I suddenly bolted and was surprised with what I had just experienced! What had just happened? What was that? I pushed him away and asked, "Who are you?" I had never experienced this before, and it was deeply moving. I questioned the closeness we were experiencing so quickly. He simply held me, and we gazed into each other's eyes with a kind of knowing from some other time. I had read of such romantic encounters, but it was new to me to have this deep embrace far different than ever before.

CHAPTER 18

Dating, Getting Acquainted, and Creating Relationship

Jim and I enjoyed going out of town for a variety of dining experiences as we continued our acquaintance. One time stands out to me: We went to a neighboring town where his oldest daughter, Claire, was in college, to treat her for dinner. After a lovely evening, we headed back home. We were in his vehicle, which was a large van, and I was aware that at times Jim would travel very near the center line or cross over it occasionally. He had had some wine with dinner, but we were busy talking and perhaps he was a bit distracted from watching the road.

Then Jim glanced at me and announced that a police officer was flashing his lights behind us to pull us over. He turned to me and said, "He's going to ask me to walk a line, which will be fine, but also to recite the alphabet and I am unable to do that accurately. I'm very dyslexic and can't get through the middle of it." I later learned that the "L-M-N-O-P" portion always stumped him. He explained later that, during his childhood, he had trouble hearing it and saying it back and visually could not see the letters for a long time.

The officer approached and asked him to step out of the van. I saw in the rearview mirror that he was asked to walk the line in the center of the road, and I waited for his return. After several minutes I wondered what was keeping us here at the side of the road. As I watched, I saw them thoroughly engaged in a conversation. It didn't look threatening, but they were still talking after twenty or thirty minutes. He returned to tell me of his venture with the officer and his explanation of not being able to recite the alphabet. The officer asked him what he did for a living. He was surprised to learn that Jim was a high school mathematics teacher and wanted to know how he had accomplished it. It turned out that the officer's son was dyslexic, and he wanted to know how he could help him. He was asking for Jim's experience and guidance.

Jim told him that he had been unable to read and learn as a young boy, but there was no awareness of dyslexia at that time. His parents had sent him to a military school where students had to march every morning, and he eventually learned how significant that was for his learning through the crossover exercise for his right and left brain coordination. All he knew then was that he felt compelled to learn to make his parents feel better about him. His parents had felt helpless and turned to this possible assistance. They didn't really tell him why at the time, but he knew of his mother crying at not being able to help him see the letters that made up the words and being unable to read like his peers. His dad also knew that when he sat down to play chess with him, Jim could be brilliant with seeing the strategy and often win the game against his father, who was educated as an engineer. His father wanted to have a place for his son that gave more hope than the school program that said he could learn a trade someday.

Jim then spoke of his own son, Troy, who had been recognized to have some early learning difficulty. Jim's wife had done some research and found a center in Chicago that did extensive testing to clarify the issues. He then also completed the testing with his son for some guidance. They had worked on it together, received some new information for greater understanding and used nutritional/supplemental assistance as was recommended for help.

He shared that later he learned of the educational kinesiology approach called Brain Gym for kids and had incorporated the four-and-a-half minute exercise with his students in his math classroom. The focus was to bring the energy of the nervous system back up into the right and left hemisphere of the brain after sitting most of the day feeling shut down. It was accomplished by doing some crossover movement with the right hand to the left knee and then left hand to the right knee for a couple of minutes along with some additional holds to anchor the energy for learning. This activity then stimulates the corpus callosum (the bundle of nerve fibers that connects the right and left brain) to bring the energy back up. As the teacher, he could once again get their attention focused for learning. The students thought it was cool and just one of the ways Mr. Daily made the classroom for advanced math interesting and fun. He became aware that this was what the marching had done for him many years before. The officer was interested and grateful.

Over the years we moved forward to support our new love affair by furthering our relationship skills and awareness with more Insight trainings and activities. Through this workshop, programs offered in Spiritual Psychology and Soul-Centered Living through the University of Santa Monica (USM) that was to be held in Philadelphia. It was the last opportunity to attend in the eastern half of the nation, before all the classes would return to Los Angeles, where the course had originated. The chancellor of the program was John-Roger, the spiritual director of the MSIA and co-creator of the Insight trainings. We were both interested in attending: Jim for a master's degree and his work with the students, and I for some healthy spiritual counseling and support with the children.

We were now engaged in this spiritual direction to live more fully from our hearts and wanted to expand our skills with this focus of wisdom. It was a welcome focus for Heartfelt Listening and seeing the Loving Essence in ourselves and the people and situations around us. We were living together at this time and felt a deep commitment to healing our past hurts and knew that we wanted more if we were to be together for a longer period. It was a sensitive time for Jim, healing from a painful divorce after seventeen years, and for myself after the sudden death of my daughter. We were committed to finding a way to be together without creating hurtful circumstances for each other. So together we chose to make the flight to Philadelphia to attend this program once a month for the next two years.

The opportunity in these off-campus USM classes was very experiential. In fact, the adventure of it lined up in a very interesting way. Jim was teaching at his Galesburg High School classroom, and once a month we flew from Kalamazoo directly to Philadelphia. He left school early, where I picked him up on Friday, and we drove directly to the airport with our written, completed homework and got onto the flight shortly before the doors closed for departure. After landing, we took a cab to the hotel and entered the classroom shortly after it had started. We immediately sat down to begin our spiritual psychology counseling skills class for the weekend. At the end of the weekend class time we needed to depart a bit early to make the flight home so we could both get to work again on Monday morning.

This grace-filled routine worked every weekend of class. The flight attendant knew we would be arriving before the doors had to close on the designated weekend, taxi transport was quickly available, and we dropped our luggage inside the doors of the hotel conference room for class, laid our homework on the readers' table, and took our seats. Class was already in session. Sharing amongst students regarding the home studies of the month was in session with the founders and facilitators, Drs. Ron and Mary Hulnick. Next, a new counseling skill was introduced. We then moved into groups of three to participate in the experience and practice with it. It was a process of ongoing awakening to the strength of who we are with new skills for letting go of the past, healing with self-forgiveness and loving, and finding in the moment a new way of being. It was really an exhilarating time of building our relationship, with all this inner healing work that came before each of us individually and then sharing it together.

One incident stands out to me that added some excitement during one afternoon's deliberate protocol of travel. We had to pick up Jim's typed copy of homework from the local university student prior to boarding the flight. His dyslexia made it a challenge to write his expressions accurately, so Jim hired this wonderful Western Michigan University student who would transcribe his heartfelt message and provide copy exactly as Jim would have said it. So we met and hurried, with both of us driving our own cars. I encouraged him to follow me as I was good at getting through traffic, and said I would get us there on time.

So we raced above the speed limit down the one-way street with no apparent traffic, and next thing I knew, we had a police officer behind us with flashing lights pulling both of us over. This time tickets were handed out, and I then learned that Jim had never been given a traffic ticket of any kind during his entire life! I felt like Eve, who had led Adam to the forbidden apple. The whole ticket thing was not new to me, nor was it foreign to me to drive with the clear intention of using the road freely if no one else was there. I was alert, quick to respond, and often exceeded the speed limit by a bit. Guilty! Jim, however was incredibly forgiving and without accusation or resentment. He never spoke negatively of what had happened or conveyed distaste to anyone that I knew of. We were still fairly new in our relationship and his forgiveness was held silently. I was forever sorry for creating this stain on his record and eternally grateful for his silent acceptance of our process with it. We had to proceed efficiently to the airport to catch our flight, and the officer graciously allowed for us to be on our way. It was a meaningful lesson for both of us!

Among the abundance of courses and many tools and guidance, one course that was key for us showed up with the relationship class from the work of Dr. Harville Hendrix and his book, *Getting the Love You Want.* After some processing and a great deal of appreciation for the healing tools he counsels for partnership, we wanted to know more. We discovered that his headquarters were in Chicago, not far from us. We chose to attend a weekend workshop with this author to see what might be in store for us. We were mesmerized with the direction and the strength of the course interaction for couples.

At the very beginning, we learned that we all choose the perfect mate who will inevitably bring forward the most challenging issue that we most want healed with the loving we have confessed for each other. When he first said it, he stated, "We will all marry the enemy, the one who will purposely bring up our greatest hurts." I was immediately shocked, and he had my attention! He had just brought up my worst fear, and I was ready instantly to step outside and vomit! My stomach was truly rebelling as I held on to my seat. We then heard how our partner, with loving compassion and understanding, with a series of active listening skills and certain responses, could provide the counsel and healing love that we all wanted in a relationship. (Thus *Getting the Love We Want.*)

We pursued this practice for the entire weekend where we actually had the experience and learned to be counselors for each other! The results filled us with reassurance for creating a partnership relationship. Jim and I found the healing within for each other, and we knew what to do in a loving and nurturing manner without blame or accusation. We continued to practice and found a new safety in taking responsibility for our own issues that would normally be projected outward with blame and hurt. Now we had tools to receive counsel from each other for our own inner healing from the experiences of fear we all bring forward from our past. They were simple and powerful skills of listening with feedback and steps for action to reverse the images of hurt. It is referred to as *imago therapy*, and we held on to this source. It was unanimous: we imported this counsel into our marriage vows as our safety net for an honoring and respect that would carry us into the long-standing relationship that we had both looked for.

The guidelines for our marriage that we accompanied with these skills were those that our attendance at MSIA had introduced us to and the Insight trainings and MSIA teachings had reinforced. They are very thoughtful and inclusive:

1. Take care of yourself so you can then care for others.
2. Don't hurt yourself, and don't hurt others.
3. Use every situation for your learning, growth, and advancement.

I mentioned these with greater detail of description early on in this memoir, but they became integral again to our continued support for our selves and each other in relationship. There is a great deal of practical content in these three statements involving caring for and not hurting self and others within all the dimensions of our physical, mental, and emotional ways of existing and relating. We used the skills of listening and healing for all these types of challenges and issues that began to show up.

We married, we continued our course work, and then we went into service with this movement of growth by sharing the teachings with weekly cassette and videotaped seminars in our home. We were delighted to have others join us in an atmosphere of this giving and receiving of Spirit. We chose to minister to our selves and others with this Spiritual focus as partners with God and shared this gift of grace as we continued on our forever opportunities of learning.

CHAPTER 19

Creating a Spiritual Marriage and Healing the Past

The spiritual focus held in these places of learning was what lifted me with my healing for clearing all of the victim, guilt, and painful grieving of Emily's passing. Jim was incredibly compassionate about this process for me. I was and am incredibly grateful for all these experiences that he enabled for us.

One most loving gift from Jim was a moment when he let me know that even though he had never met my daughter, Emily, he truly had come to love her as I do. It was a moment of compassion that I would never had thought to ask for, but he graciously gave it for me to receive. I felt a deep acceptance for myself and my process of recovery! What a beautiful awareness that this companionship that we were developing was so expansive and inclusive of God's Loving without borders or restrictions! He had come to know Em from my sharing and from within and let me know of it. My heart was enlarged and swollen with the loving of it.

As we proceeded through our classes, a project was required where we were to identify a desire, a personal wish containing a great challenge that we could turn from a perceived impossibility into a possibility. Jim's cherished idea was to be comfortable in depths of water to be able to snorkel and scuba dive and see underwater. Jim held several barriers to this ability. Jim had accumulated many fears over the years from childhood due to his inability to see clearly. He had a severe visual disability, with a prescription of 20/800. He was nearly blind without his corrective lenses, which kept him from learning to swim, let alone go underwater with any thought of seeing. Although he grew up on a lake, he could not swim. The vision limitations he had grown up with brought many fears and challenges that he knew he would need to overcome.

His sister Cleora had learned of a doctor in California who was doing radial keratotomy; a procedure that changed the surface of the lens of the eye, correcting the projection of light on the retina, which would eliminate his need for glasses! He had a complete trust in his sister and her resources and he immediately grabbed on to the opportunity. He was amazed and startled by the possibility of correction for clear vision. We made arrangements and flew to Long Beach, CA and in four days both eyes were corrected, and he had 20/20 vision!

It was granted! After more than forty years of compensating and making alterations for living, he could now see perfectly as he had never seen before! He was told that over the years this perfect correction might relax to some need for glasses; a few years later this did come true, but to go from 20/800 to this incredible correction was a huge recovery! There was a whole new view of life for him to check out and recreate perceptions that he had held for years! For sure, the potential for swimming and preparing for underwater snorkeling and scuba diving was still a journey away, but it was within sight! He had taken a huge first step! He was awed and amazed by this gift to see the world accurately without the heavy bottle-bottom lenses of so many past years.

Next, he initiated swimming lessons at the local YMCA. He took the beginner class <u>three</u> times with a super supportive coach who admired his fortitude and direction. He spoke of the teamwork with this gentleman who took on the project to get Jim to the underwater goal of scuba diving. He pressed on.

A great fear came up when he got into the pool to rehearse the scuba technique he would need to go underwater, take off the diver's mask, clear it, and then replace it and restore the breathing technique. It would mean opening his eyes underwater, where he had never seen before, and trust a vision that he had never had for his first forty-four years! It was an experience of anxiety that he had not known before and required that he bring up a longevity of fears that he would not have known to face without this gift of newly found vision. He worked the course again and again with perseverance, determination, and supportive leadership and healing counsel. He wrote and processed with the many therapeutic approaches presented to us every weekend in the monthly spiritual psychology class, tracking his process and progress with baby steps to the eventual final test.

He arrived to do the underwater dive for his completion exam in the murky waters of the clearest lake in our vicinity that this local course could provide outside of the pool. He spoke of the clouded water from the windy conditions of that day and losing sight of his classmates. But pushing on, he demonstrated stepping through his fears and completed the requirements for scuba certification! He received his document and became a swimmer and a diver complete with all the gear and skill for the graduating performance! Within himself Jim had qualified with honors for his master's degree in spiritual psychology accompanied with the experience of his newfound vision and skills.

Although Jim rarely shared verbally in the USM classes regarding the goals and direction he was taking, he sincerely moved into the loving essence for himself with this sense for re-visioning the world around him. It was my privilege to be a witness of his process.

As I look back on it now, I am aware that the expansiveness of this eye-opening experience really had many more dimensions than I ever consciously thought of during that time. I wonder how much came to him and how it was all manifesting with eyes that could see anew with more dimension than just through the corrective lenses that he wore for so many years. I do know that at his retirement he was empowered to proclaim himself a professional tennis player! He had played for years before at the indoor courts in Kalamazoo and had coached the students at the high school for many years. When we moved to Gulf Shores, he upped his time at playing the game, and daily he talked of his match of the day: how he saw the ball coming, how he received the ball to his racquet, his expertise or lack thereof of executing his return, and then his overall scores in relation to the camaraderie of the players. His game always had variables that he contemplated for his awareness and the next opportunity. He planned to master the game and make it to the seventy-and-over doubles national championship games with his buddies from the Gulf Shores Peninsula Tennis Club. He had moved into retirement and had the perfect setup and competition for making the progress to his goal. The men there were on board, and they often made it to the state and regional playoffs.

Jim had completed his years of teaching, and we had made our move. He had enjoyed his thirty-three years at Galesburg-Augusta High School in Michigan, and with the surmounting stressors of that environment he had purchased and opted out for early retirement. He had been granted Honorary Teacher of the Year seven out of the last ten years of his teaching, as voted upon by the student population, but was now having difficulty with students who had no awareness of advanced math but were being placed in his classroom due to a shortage of classrooms.

He was part of a small educational community, and funds and classrooms had been cut. The teachers made efforts to mentor these kids, and Jim spoke of one student of his concern who he discovered had been living in his car for three months after his stepmother disowned him. This was after his father left him under prior conditions. The actual whereabouts of the mother was unknown. There were other examples of this sort that made teaching with family support and guidance impossible. This adolescent teen was left with a lack of interest and supportive encouragement in an inappropriate classroom placement that created further failure, disapproval, and abandonment of ability for himself. Jim knew that at one time this student was a smart kid. It was a defeating situation and circumstance for teaching. Jim was ready for retirement. The classroom no longer held the environment for learning that he had designed as his purpose for service. There were parents who begged him to stay, but the number of students in the classroom with the ability to learn was rapidly diminishing.

One day I was able to watch the scenarios that Jim had always described to me. It was the year of Jim's birthday which occurred during classroom time. Most years it arrived during spring break when we would fly to Florida to be with his father, whose birthday fell two days after his. But this last year of teaching his birthday was during school. I arranged with the principal of the school, who was a close buddy of Jim's, to arrive with cake and candles to share with the classes. The students assisted with a banner to hang outside the door to pull off the surprise event. After a quick celebration with each class singing and sharing a small piece of cake, I went to the back corner of the room.

The classroom seating was typical, with light-colored wooden desks with armrests on the side for writing and the black slate chalkboard up front across the entire wall. The adjacent wall directly across from the hall entry exhibited a project by an art student in his class. This young woman had produced an honorary piece for Mr. D (as Jim was known). It was a portrait wall with drawings of Pythagoras, Einstein, and Mr. D. Mr. D was centered between the brilliance of these two famous scholars. Jim was humbled and honored by this display.

After the initial birthday acknowledgment, the class lesson

was presented. I watched as Mr. D regrouped the attention of the class on the next skill for geometry, algebra, trigonometry, or calculus. It was mostly as he described, but the part that really held my awe was how he maneuvered and held their attention or would redirect the energy of the classroom and recommit the students to hear what he was saying. He used the brilliance of the students to come up with how to assist the student who was having trouble in the next desk. He helped them see the dynamics of the other students and how to give and get help to work the problems for themselves. They thrived through finding out how their classmates got it and how they could also see it. He also kept the process going, always first reviewing where they'd left off the day before so that it would be easy to move to the next skill. It would be easy and fun, he assured them, because of what they had learned the day before. He continued being a principal resource or support, stabilized them with their experience, and then began the new skill. This is what the students talked about when they nominated him for teacher of the year.

Then came the last end-of-day class that I had heard so much about. They didn't and couldn't sit or be still! They moved in and out of their seats, standing, walking, and talking or were simply up and down in their assigned seats. Jim told jokes, got them laughing to find their attention, and then at the moment of grasping it, he slipped in the information and got them moving on it. I watched in amazement as I saw him redirect the seeming inattentiveness of the students. It was clear that I would *not* be the right person to teach and accept the behaviors I saw and still think that I could teach. Jim seemed to observe, grasp, and move with it all and punched in the information, building their abilities and skills to learn!

The students loved Mr. D. They told me how he taught them about the presence of energy by creating a ball between their hands. It was very cool to them! They could bring the palms of their hands together without touching and feel the warmth and tingle between them to create that ball of space that existed there; representing something that couldn't be seen as real. The numbers seemed to be representation of the movement of energy; a reflection they could manifest on paper as they learned to work their equations. That's what I saw!

Jim had other physiological challenges besides learning with dyslexia. There were some physical body care needs as well. Jim and I met as middle-aged adults. He had already run the NY marathon in his earlier years and now was playing tennis several times a week. It was apparent to me that he had some curvatures in his back and now some joint discomforts. He solicited regular chiropractic care; he had a kyphosis in his upper back and a scoliosis on the lower back and a place in the lumbar spine that was what I called as a pediatric nurse a pre-bifida place, much like the spinal bifida I had seen with some children that were born with this condition. It was like a beginning of the vertebral opening of the spinal cord. He was also challenged with an ongoing cough that seemed primarily stimulated with eating.

At the same time, while in Kalamazoo, Jim and I participated regularly with ongoing MSIA seminars and other spiritual retreats as they became available in the Kalamazoo and Chicago area. As we both became more engaged with the people in this practice, we also heard more about the alternative and complementary modalities for health and healing.

As a professional in pediatric nursing and a child life specialist, I utilized services other than the medical analysis and treatment already being provided. These modalities included psychological visualization for reducing and eliminating fear and pain, guided imagery for receiving IV therapy without pain, play therapy to replicate procedures such as casting and shots, pet therapy without dander or feathers with a local zoo, music therapy from the local Western Michigan University intern students, and parental and peer support for normalizing daily living with provisions for maintaining school educational goals and parent attendance 24/7.

At this time, in the early 1990s the director of music therapy from the local university asked me if she could offer me a practice session for her new work with healing with a more specific and individualized type of sound therapy. Different than the music therapy that the children were receiving from her student population, it was individually orchestrated by recording the tones of a person's energy from a voice graph spoken into a microphone transmitted through a piano tuner. From this projection she created a graph display of my physically transmitted energy by musical notes. I could see on the graph which frequencies of sound vibration were present or absent from the musical scale of notes. It was very engaging and caught my curiosity for health and healing.

I had experienced a skiing injury, and she had noted the discomfort in my left knee and the ensuing arthritic type reaction I was having. She wanted to see if sound could be healing. I was willing and wondered what this would be like. As she transmitted some sound formulations through a bass speaker system, I was to give feedback about whether I experienced any sensation. At one point I felt a vibration or tingling sensation in my knee that was actually very comforting, and as she turned off the transmission I could tell that I wanted it back! It felt good to have it on! That was what she was looking for. She in turn recorded this sound onto a cassette or videotape so I could then treat myself in my home with the nurturing frequency of that "sound formula."

The sound frequency formula was created with the tones that were stressed out as shown on the graph. She had designed a combination of two tones dialed into a tone box that delivered a standing wave form using the octaves of the alpha, beta, theta, and delta levels for a connection to the brain receptors for returning the stressed out energy/frequency. This particular designated note combination was what I experienced as comfort to my painful arthritic knee. I was merely to play the recorded tape in my home (I didn't need to actually hear it), and my body would receive the transmission and send that healing vibration to where it was needed. There was no actual scientific reason for this mode of transmission; it was still only theorized, and we were some of the first recipients to have some experience with it.

It turned out that Jim, who was curious but said nothing regarding what I was being offered, also observed that his joints, particularly his knee, which was always in pain the morning after his tennis play, was no longer swollen with pain! As we inquired further into this work, I chose, with Jim's support, to learn and also become a practitioner.

A next occurrence for alternative help was a referral to a homeopathic practitioner who was an engineer. He evaluated the need for service by taking Polaroid pictures of the client in his treatment room where he had installed a null field generator. If the picture appeared unclear; blurry, and unfocused, he would muscle test your body with kinesiology to see where the issue was and bring into your body field a homeopathic substance that could be of assistance. Then with the strength of your body response with muscle testing, he would take another photo and see if your energy field was clear with a focused picture by simply holding the bottle to your body. When the picture became clear, he would then again ask the body with muscle testing how much and how often. Jim and I each found ways of being more comfortable in our body with the use of this assistance—particularly Jim, who would have less coughing.

The coughing was a recurring issue. We then worked with a nutritional practitioner who again did muscle testing and was led to a protocol with foods and teas. Jim's body seemed very favorable to this prescribed food protocol. A seven-month protocol was created with a different food or tea substance for each month. There were teas, greens, and herbs to be used for a month at a time along with his regular diet. While doing so on a daily basis, Jim was totally clear of his coughing or the frequent tightening of his throat. He chose not to do it one day when he was getting frustrated with how long it went on, and sure enough the uncomfortable and sometimes gagging cough resumed. So he reengaged in the protocol, resulting in the absence of cough and throat discomfort. After he finished the protocol, Jim was clear of the threatening cough during or after eating for a year or more.

Over the years we continued to keep our eyes and ears open to measures and ways of health care for prevention and reversal of any uncomfortable symptoms in our body. Being a nurse and also interested in the psychological, nutritional, and exercising measures for health care, I became more and more engaged with alternative modalities. Being involved in pediatrics and the fearful and painful events that occurred in hospital care, I saw how visualizations could totally reverse the hydrotherapy pain for a child who was debriding skin tissue from an electrical accident. I watched children find acceptance and peace while visualizing their chemotherapy work through their blood vessels like Pac-men or Pac-girls. I saw children find joy and comfort during many painful and fearful procedures by having the time and tools for play and keeping a family member in total attendance 24/7.

I witnessed a baby who was at death's door resume breathing as the doctors resuscitated with little hope while the parents and I prayed fervently in the next room for God's intervention. I saw a parent who left our services with her child diagnosed with a brain tumor and no help available return a couple of months later to share that they had chosen to leave the country for alternative treatment, and now the brain tumor was gone. It opened my mind to wondering how and wanting to find *more* of what must be available outside the medical domain of hospital services for care and healing.

I was now engaging spiritually with the expansion of possibilities to an inner awareness of wisdom from the Heart that reminded me of Jesus the Christ's words when He spoke and said, "This that I do you too shall do and even greater," in reference to the healing power of love and touch. I wanted to know more of what that content would be. Jim and I were in daily practice with the inner guidance of spirit, and when avenues of healing were shared with us that others were experiencing, we were willing to check them out.

I was guided to a former friend of my childhood who was involved in alternative care that she had pursued for her own complicated health needs. She was using a microscope assessment tool with a droplet of blood sample, that was actually attached to a videotaping camera and TV screen to record the sample to take home as a follow-up reference. We were able to see the movement and cellular function of our blood cells. She had pictures of different ways of occlusion or clotting that the body may be experiencing directly in the blood vessel circulation that could be seen on the video screen from the microscope. She would then offer some herbal supplements and enzymes to assist digestion and anti-inflammatory treatment.

It became apparent to Jim and me that we were harboring lots of rouleau formation or clotted blood cells that were indicative of inflammation. She said it was a very common view of what she found in most all of the clients who were checking out this work. We began to use the supplements that would assist this issue for us and found again more comfort. There was a particular anti-inflammatory formula that was a compilation of a mega amount of enzyme that was very efficient for me with symptoms of arthritis that were beginning to manifest. My mom had significant arthritis in her hands and other joints so that they were becoming deformed, and I was seeing some initial manifestation of the same. I was now continuing the use of sound therapy, but some of the symptoms persisted. We could actually see it here in this microscopic viewing and the taping of it that we had acquired. This anti-inflammatory enzymatic formulation was magnificent in clearing the rouleau and could be *seen* within ten to twenty minutes with the microscopic projection after we took the capsules orally with water. The blood cells were now free flowing in the circulation sample with the microscopic viewing! My pain was alleviated.

We spent some years with this supplemental support when my childhood friend—also named Judy and also a nurse—became acquainted with an exciting piece of information about the ongoing formation of autoimmune inflammation. She had been introduced to the research and nutritional information from the book, *Eat Right 4 (for) Your Type* by Dr. Peter D'Adamo. The research directed us to the foods that created the inflammation so that they could be avoided, thereby giving individuals the power from their own homes to purchase foods that were compatible to reverse inflammatory conditions!

It described the process of incompatibility of *some foods* that created inflammation in the blood circulation according to the blood type antigens' protective response. It was described as the lectin response. It became known that there were some foods, according to this genetic immune response that is our blood type inheritance, that are *not* recognized as an actual food, but a foreign substance. Our own blood type antigen protection of our individual blood type is meant to fight it off, much as it would if it were a bacterial, viral, or parasitic antagonist.

Judy begged me to join her to help others who have these ongoing inflammatory issues to engage in this practice of blood type awareness. Being licensed nurses, we were able to do this droplet test for blood type testing and together with the recipient reap the results to educate for this home healing tool. We could actually reverse and prevent inflammatory discomfort without the use of anti-inflammatory drugs or other aids.

At the time of this discovery in 1998, two years after publication, this book was at the top of the *New York Times* best seller list for health literature and then stayed there for many months and in the top fifty for many years. By this time I was in serious joint pain from the time I woke up in the morning until bedtime. The joints in my hands were enlarged and reddened just as my mother's had been, and I could no longer lift the weight of my cooking pans. I had gotten the vacuum sweeper with the special handle for arthritis, and I was on my way to the handicapped condition of my mother.

Judy called to say, "Judy, Judy, we have to do this work!" I got the book, and I proceeded to eat explicitly as directed for my blood type, A! I had been in this ongoing pain for nearly a year, and I jumped into the program 100 percent. I wanted to see if what she was saying was true! Even though I did not even know all of the identified foods, I managed to avoid those on the "avoid" list to see how my body would respond. By the fifth day, before the week was over, I was without any pain! The red, swollen joints had resolved, and the morning-to-evening pain was gone! It was an actual miracle visited upon me by my own choice and actions. I heard that voice, *This that I do you too shall do and even greater.* I continued and I no longer had the swollen joints and the pain in all of my joints as I formerly experienced.

I was grateful beyond words and continued religiously on this prescription for my health care with the pure motivation that I was no longer in any pain. The additional benefits were mere side effects for me after this initial response. I had gained weight to the tune of ten pounds a year for the last few years, with my hormone response in synchrony with menopause. Jim and I exercised six days a week with a disciplined and trainer-guided program, and my weight only varied by one to three pounds. Now with this new food protocol for my blood type, I was releasing two pounds a week, and it continued for eight weeks and then slowed down to just gradual weight loss. I did not eat less but simply made the choices that were compatible for me with the genetics of my blood type. I was at that time prone to sinus pressure and pain. It was nonexistent from this time forward. I also found that for my type, different than the other types; soy was very beneficial. I sought out organic soy products only, as was recommended, and, with a daily dose of tofu, reversed all of my hot sweats during the day and night. Life in this body was happy again!

Jim's blood type was different than mine. So we looked closely at the food recommendations for his genetic inheritance. There were foods that he too was eating regularly with the ongoing assumption that the healthy choices we were making were surely good for us, only to discover again that some of our food choices were not the healthy resource that we wanted. We were blessed by this guidance to know our bodies more purely with the opportunity to honor ourselves with joy and gratitude as the vessels of God's Spirit.

Jim came to know what was creating the tightness in his throat and what foods would manifest that response. Some foods were easy to give up. Others were not. We did continue to use our enzymes simply due to the process of cooking which removes some of the enzymes supplied by raw food, but we definitely found more comfort with eating and had a choice for health and wellness that was very empowering for prevention and reversal of disease symptoms.

CHAPTER 20

The Tennis Professional

Jim continued his chosen career for retirement as a self-proclaimed professional tennis player with the troupe of men at our local tennis club on the Gulf coast. We played on soft rubico clay courts to keep our joints as comfortable as possible with this ongoing exercise, and Jim's custom was to come home and describe his best play of each day. He had continued his chiropractic care with our locally loved chiropractic neurologist, and he had done an intensive type of massage called *Rolfing* for releasing chronic constriction in his spinal muscles from ongoing spinal challenge to assist his posturing.

He was doing well on the courts. His team had won the local competition and the state competition several times, and he pursued his vision to make it to the national championship in his category of play. Some of his teammates had approached national championships in younger years, so the ongoing play was purposeful with a great deal of mutual camaraderie. Jim had a wicked return of serve with a chop and spin; he sent the ball in unknown directions that I always heard about from his opponents. Then he would describe his other returns and how he saw them coming at him or not. Whether it was a good day or not so good on the court, he would again analyze it for preparation of the next day's play.

But at one point he came home and said that he was losing sight of the ball in his peripheral vision. He had told our chiropractic neurologist friend about it. The doctor recommended a list of herbs and supplements that Jim could try. "Hmm …," I said to myself. At this time I had become quite educated regarding the blood type nutrition and the common genetic predispositions of health issues for each blood type and knew that fine neurological issues would be the most common to show up with aging for Jim's blood type, B. I was also aware that Jim had dug in his heels regarding a couple of the more common foods in our diet that were restricted for blood type B. He had been unwilling to give up especially chicken and corn, two big foods that are not compatible with his type. He was determined to have his theater popcorn if we went to see a movie, which we enjoyed most every week, and chicken whenever he wanted it.

The work of adding more supplements was on my plate, not his. I was the one who coordinated delivering all our supplements, and now he wanted to add more! This was my time for showing up with some resistance. I was not willing to add more until we checked out his willingness to experiment by doing without the corn and chicken to see if they were the cause of his detriment. He was manifesting the perfection of his blood type B diet, and I wanted him to have all the benefits of the researched information. He agreed to the test. He went without the chicken and corn, and to his amazement his peripheral vision returned! This was a serious self-clinical discovery, since it was crucial for his "professional" tennis game. He resumed with expertise to his team. He maintained and even elevated his level of play on the courts, thankful all over again for his vision and the scope of it.

Jim was also watching the pressure in his eyes. When we met, he had an ongoing pressure measurement in both eyes that was borderline for a diagnosis of glaucoma. Each year with his vision checkup, he would have his pressures checked. It occurred that this pressure measurement went up, and a prescription for medication was recommended. He wanted to avoid this treatment since he knew that it did not reverse the symptoms and that eventually it meant he would go blind. He wanted another course.

He was referred to a physician who was also well qualified with Asian acupuncture. This doctor had studied many years in China and knew all the medical protocols as well. Jim chose this avenue. This doctor also required that Jim stay connected with his ophthalmologist to track their progress and get regular pressure measurements. His own doctor refused to entertain Jim's choice, and we found another who would be accommodating and interested in Jim's ongoing welfare.

The protocol involved auricular and sometimes hand acupuncture treatment. We went for this procedure every other week and then monthly and we watched as his pressures were reversed from 24 and 25 (borderline glaucoma) to 14 and 15 (normal). He had totally reversed the concern for aging blindness. Three times now he had opened his vision greater than he had been born with! Through the use of care unknown or rejected by the majority of the medical model, Jim had stepped into courage to see possibilities beyond what was commonly known or unknown and created his own miracle for healing.

But our dear friend Judy was not going to forget Jim. She saw the issues in his back, and she related with some of the same challenges in her body. Her search led to a noninvasive treatment for straightening the spine from hereditary dysfunction. It involved some research and protocol with a doctor in Seattle, the use of a balloon from a finger cot inserted up the nose, and a pressure tool to move the sphenoid bone. All we heard was a "balloon up the nose," and we couldn't stop laughing! Judy must be kidding! No way would we jump into this one! But Judy persevered, and Jim's back was now causing numbness to move down his legs. He was constantly stretching and bending forward to release the pressure and keep on his feet.

The issue culminated the year that we went to New Orleans near Mardi Gras time with his sister Cleora and her partner, Robert. We hiked up and down the streets and in and out of a couple of lounges. As we moved through this territory on Bourbon Street in the French Quarter, Jim bent over every few steps to keep up with our progress. As I followed and watched from behind him, seeing my own angle on his presentation, I knew his back needed something more than his simple stretching technique. We contacted Judy, and she guided us to this outrageous service.

A single "treatment" was a complex four-day process. We prepared with an intensive session of education as to how the procedure worked, what research had been done thus far, and how treatment had evolved into the procedure we were about to receive. Once again, we were grateful to be there and check it out. It began with anatomical measurements and then engagement of balloon pressure to the sphenoid bone, reached through the nasal cavity. The pressure was set to one of sixteen fine-tuned positions, as evaluated exclusively again by kinesiology, with a very highly trained practitioner. We learned that the balance of the inner ear was directly correlated to the alignment of the spine. The movement of the sphenoid bone would open the cranium to a greater size and require the realignment of the spine as the inner ear adjusted for balance with the vertebrae of the spine.

We were both engaged in learning about the whole scope of it, but with particular attention to Jim's needs and his gradually deteriorating ability to walk. We were both willing to check out the experience of this procedure. Jim had some immediate lessening of the numbness that was going down both legs! We were excited to continue. We were told that with the four-day pressure treatments, we would continue to experience ongoing expansion of the cranium after we left for the next month. The movement of this inner ear balance would gradually help straighten the spine along with the inner ear shift of equilibrium.

Jim's condition was noticeably reversing, and we continued to engage in the work for months and then years to come. Prior to this treatment, Jim's kyphosis (hunchback) was becoming quite noticeable, and he was self-conscious about wearing a suit or sport coat. He chose a wide double-breasted model to hang well in front. After a year or so he happened to put on a jacket that we found in a fine department store sale and was moved to see that it buttoned and looked handsome on him. It was a visible measurement of this treatment's effects showing that the kyphosis had been reduced.

We were told that if we had not engaged in this protocol, he would have been in a wheelchair within months. That was not happening. We had found a preventive and reversal technique that worked. This work is called neurocranial restructuring, and we were truly grateful to our beloved Judy who joined in our laughter and did not give up on us and her caring for Jim. We were referred to a well-trained practitioner in Florida to whom we could drive every three months, and there we found wonderful support and friendship. Tennis play was back with Jim's newly strengthened body, and once again life was good.

We felt divinely directed. We were literally and figuratively creating new bodies for ourselves as we mutually found the authentic spirit of our Loving with our work with Soul Transcendence. We learned that the body is flexible and creative in majestic ways through the Light and Sound known as the infinite *Word* of God manifested through modalities of all sorts of energy through the guidance of the wisdom inherent in each of us. It is so, as our Soul attunes to the inner process to meet with the outer reality. The reflection becomes known as the Healing Source that shows up as we are open to receive.

It was a joy-filled and mystical process of discovery and growth. Our bodies were the instruments of moving inward and outward for awareness discoveries of wisdoms that were not commonly known. We were guided by those who had experienced them before us. We shared the benefit with deep gratitude. It was majestic to be a part of this movement on my spiritual inner awareness and share this journey with Jim, who was so willing to explore and enter into all the possibilities for his and my growth, learning, and upliftment. Daily we practiced going inward to the Light of the Christ and the Holy Spirit, where we attended to our connection with God through the transcending experience with our Soul. Daily we cared for the vessel of the Soul in this body as we traversed through the day in community with each other, our spiritual family, our birth families, and our friends and community. We participated to the fullest of our knowing and beyond.

This that we have done is as Christ did as He brought the Loving energy of healing with the simple outreach of His hand. We can do similar with the outreach to those who know and trust the gathering of two with like mind into all the frequencies of Loving and all its courses of manifestation. The gifts of many are brought forward so that we can all partake and know the healing course through the source within each of us. Jim and I enjoyed the partnership of this journey. It was a course accompanied with gratitude and joy along the way. He was willing to explore options for health with me as we asked for the divine guidance for healing: the healing from the deeply painful loss of a beautiful eleven-year-old daughter to the renewed meaning of an expansive life, fulfilling in ways that I would never have known to ask for. Jim was my teacher and provider to find and partake of whatever nature of healing and awakening we could consume. My gratitude of God's gifts through each of us is full. I delight in it.

CHAPTER 21

Freedom to Completion

So what did happen that Jim then passed on as he did with the expression of cancer? We had learned of the reversal of cancer as well, years earlier, after the death of my father and then the occurrence of a tumor with my mom. I know some may have asked these questions inwardly without wanting to create guilt or any further grief or pain. Why weren't we able to reverse this growth of cancer cells for Jim? What turning points entered or were allowed to culminate in meeting the end of Jim's life as it occurred?

We had lived on the tenth floor of the Orange Beach Condo for ten years, and Jim had said we would never leave. Our view of the Gulf of Mexico was a beautiful daily gift. We slept each night with the sounds of the waves hitting the white sandy shoreline. It was the same sound that I had experienced ten years before when we found this setting. I sat waiting for Jim to shower as we prepared for dinner and as I sat chose some inner meditation time when the sounds of the waves meeting the shore just simply lifted me into another realm. My spirit soared into a Light Presence, and it had become a sign for us. We had toured the coast from Florida to California, and this was the best and most beautiful setting with an optimal price.

Jim had found a great setting for tennis, with many courts available and lots of people who showed up at the courts to play. His invitation to the Peninsula Racquet Club led to the camaraderie of men with whom he spent a gracious and enjoyable ten years. He declared many times that he had been born to live and sweat on the courts in the South. It was instant companionship such as he had never known before, and he soaked it up and met with the brilliance and laughter of men who came with their lives into retirement from all walks of expertise and experiences. They all had many years to talk about and bring to the courts of their play.

More people began to discover the area, and the population grew. We had chosen to purchase a piece of property at the Peninsula Club Community, either as an investment piece or else to build on, should the beach shoreline get too crowded. It did. We began plans to build on our lot at the club where Jim and I played on the courts and socialized with many friends.

The schedule on the courts was such that you showed up every day that you wanted to play. You drew a card and headed for the designated court. Then on Saturdays the women joined in, and we played mixed doubles. I was always glad when he was on the same side of the court with me. Being across from him made returning the ball a dicey prospect.

He insisted that I could learn it and made me watch and practice it over and over. He had coerced me to play after a guest couple stayed with us one weekend, and he begged my participation so we could join our guests on our rooftop courts at the condo. He got all excited when I actually connected with the ball and sent it back.

He insisted that I was to learn tennis so we could play together. It wasn't my heart's desire, but it was for him, so I began lessons to play with the women and have more interests in common with Jim. I did get to play with the hundreds of women who enjoyed tennis in Gulf Shores and the Pensacola, Florida, area. We played in all levels of USTA leagues and enjoyed our social friendships.

For ten years we lived in the most beautiful setting, overlooking the Gulf of Mexico. After two years of wintering there from our homes in Michigan, we moved permanently to enjoy the gorgeous colors over the waters and the expansive sky of purples and blues with reflections of greens, as well as storm fronts and rains and whitecaps to accompany the winds. Each day dolphins came out from the nearby bay, passed by to eat, and then returned to the bay.

As we sat on the balcony across the front of our unit on the tenth floor, the sea gulls or pelicans would meander by with their wings flapping or just gliding across our visual field. As they became aware of us sitting at this height, their eyes would turn to us and make contact. It was a meeting of eyes that was probably the most unique for seeing the loving essence of another life in a very unexpected way. It was a comical and instant visitation, as if they were saying to us, "What are you doing up here in my flight pattern?" It was a serendipitous meeting that gave a spark of joy as it occurred.

"Hello, Mr. Pelican. Nice of you to pass by." I smiled inwardly.

One day a dolphin greeted me in another unique timing of circumstance. As I stood at the kitchen sink, I glanced left and looked directly out the glass door to the gulf to find a dolphin centered precisely in that space and standing up out of the water on her tail fin as if to greet me. I had never seen them do this as they passed by to circle around to scrounge and feed. It was as if I was watching a show of dolphins trained to stand high in the water on command, but to my amazement this dolphin did so at the moment I greeted her out the window. Or maybe I turned at the moment the dolphin spoke a greeting to me. There she was, upright and standing in center stage, framed by the doorway from where I stood. What a delight! I felt blessed with the presence of it.

We lived a full and blessed life elevated on this tenth floor of the Sea Chase Condominium complex. Jim said we would never leave, but by the time ten years rolled around, so did the crowds begin to gather. A different opportunity presented itself when I suggested to Jim that we needed to upgrade our bath facilities and suggested some stonework for enlarging our showers. He resisted and said to check with our former manager, Jimmy. He had become a successful realtor and good friend and would advise us. He told us to do nothing, and he could sell our unit for a huge amount of money, in fact, triple what we'd paid for it!

We thought he was making a joke and began to laugh. He wasn't joking. In two weeks he had the offer for us. Jim said we couldn't afford to stay, and we began our home contracting plans to build on our Peninsula Mobile Bay lot. We in turn bought a simple small 600+ square foot condo unit a few miles down the beach while formulating plans to fit the Peninsula lot and our desires for enjoying that area.

CHAPTER 22

Hurricane Evacuation

Six weeks later Hurricane Ivan came along directly overhead and surrounding us and we no longer had a place to live. We had evacuated ASAP with everyone else, forming perfect cooperation and movement with all of the inhabitants of the island, and headed north up the Alabama inland area, only to meet a gridlock on Interstate Highway 10. Jim and I were caravanning with our two vehicles, and Jim phoned me and said, "Get out the map and get us out of here!"

I looked and said, "Okay, we are taking this next exit and will be seeing parts of Alabama that we have never seen before!" About a dozen other cars followed us, and everyone else stayed in the gridlock for many more hours. Our MSIA extended family was waiting for us in Birmingham, and we arrived eight hours later via back roads and hills. A trip that is normally four hours was completed through crisis and grace in eight hours. The storm wiped out the coastline and moved the shoreline an entire mile inland, to the border of the Peninsula Community on Fort Morgan Road. Two weeks later we were allowed to return, and friends from Michigan told us to stay in their home at the Peninsula Development. The Peninsula Resort was the only place where power had stayed on throughout the hurricane event. This is where our lot was that we were to build our next home.

As we drove in for our inspection, the roads were cleared, but the accumulated trash on both sides of the road was piled higher than our vehicles. I thought that this must be what a war zone looked like. For weeks there were semi-truck sized trash services gathering the road debris. As soon as they moved through the piles and cleared the way, the next layer of trash and debris reaccumulated. The sign for us to find the open driveway to enter the Peninsula grounds was a blue rowboat that had landed there, pointed upward from the force of Ivan's wind and water.

The devastation of the properties was massive and disheartening. We were finally able to take a boat ride to the shoreline to see the condo unit where we had relocated. The waters had not receded, so it would be a while until we were able to actually visit the premises. Our 1980s-era two-story building was still standing, as it was basically protected by the tall brick condo next to us.

Our unit was in the back third of the development. The front units had been totally pulled apart by the water and winds. The remainder of the buildings had the air conditioners stripped off, and the asphalt pavement for all our roadways and parking spaces was totally lifted from under the building! Some places in the asphalt were actually bubbled up like a soft gel! It was an astounding view of the power of the hurricane winds and water! It was an unimaginable sight! The people of gulf shores who had lived through many storms just proceeded to clean it up. The work was an ongoing ordeal of picking up debris and throwing it into the next truck bed that passed by as if on an unending conveyor belt.

After the first month our friends also came back to view the damage, and we then started our series of five moves before we chose to get to higher ground in Birmingham. We were told that our condo would be ready for occupation in three months, so we found a rental on the premises there in Peninsula that was available for three months. But the powers that held the insurance monies for the recovery did not release the funds, and the governor and the US president had to step in to mandate their release to the owners and contractors who had already prepared their bids for recovery.

Three months had passed, and now we needed to find another rental. Places were not easy to find. Everyone was in the same boat that we were. The unit next to us was for sale and Jim and I thought about purchasing it, which turned out to be a welcome and less costly outlay than renting. However, it would not be available for another month. We found a not-so-desirable unit to rent for a month and moved in. And then we moved again to the purchased condo. Our furniture from the original sale had been put into storage, so we again got the movers to assist and get moved in.

After a few months the property values went up again. It was a surprising amount and we were suddenly in the realty business. We had property we could not build on because there was no insurance available to secure our property value. Local property values had now doubled and tripled. We had been informed that the retired military population, some from the nearby naval base, were the only population who could access insurance. We were on two waiting lists without any hope for it to change. God's grace had already been present and abundant for us. We started selling it all, and because we found ourselves in Birmingham more often than we'd expected, we felt drawn to an area built as a traditional neighborhood development that was totally delightful and suited to our needs. What if we just relocated to higher ground? Multiple hurricane threats to the coast had been predicted, and without insurance to support our plans for building, we chose to sell and move on.

It was a huge financial gain and also a huge loss for Jim. He announced that we had taken in more money in that year than he had ever experienced in all his years of investment. At the same time, he would be losing all his tennis comrades with this move. We checked the courts and clubs in the area of the TND, learned of the big activity in that area for tennis, and decided we could do it. We already researched all of the interior design and appliances that we wanted in a home with Jim's best friend, a contractor and builder. This new home would now be a Craftsman style, a departure from the furnishings and colors we had used in the more tropical area of the southern beach. We would have to check it out and see what would open up for us. We placed our concerns into God's Loving Light and asked once again for divine direction and grace. It had already been given in ways that were surprising and totally serendipitous. Some that were outstanding were:

1. Our courage to sell the condo that created a multiple income above the initial cost of our investment. We had just completed holding the two-year Master's of Spiritual Science (MSS) class in our home on the tenth floor. This spiritual coordinate seems significant to mention here, as our physical environment made a huge movement from this point on. John Morton, the spiritual director, had come for a wonderful sharing with the sweet small group of participants and facilitators who traveled monthly for two years. Our lives were enriched in many ways of multidimensional spirituality. Jim and I came into a renewal of our marriage that he personally announced during our course work. It was a beautiful gift of our growth and commitment together. The movement of our spiritual inner awareness had experienced a beautiful growth as well as the outer expression of our lives together.

   The sale of our condominium in the midst of a large realty growth spurt was massively persuasive to Jim who had said we would never depart from this site. With this offer he admitted we couldn't afford not to move.

2. We quickly found a small condo unit to live in, now 10 years later at the same cost as when we first bought our Sea Chase Unit. An evident economy shift. We lived there for six weeks before Hurricane Ivan came through. The Sea Chase Condo we had just left had devastating damage that led to lawsuits regarding structural issues and years of assessment costs that came to more than eighty thousand dollars for each inhabitant. They were the last development on the beach to be repaired. We had departed six weeks before Ivan and bypassed this trauma and delay.

3. Finding housing in the area was impossible for most. Our first offer was a phone call from friends in Michigan who would not be using their home at Peninsula for another month. We were welcome to be there. The second arrived while I played a tennis match prior to the end of our month. A team member said they could not use the condo offered them because their insurance would not finance what they needed. I asked if we could be considered, and the personal referral was provided. I checked with our insurance company on the way home and found that we had the coverage. *Another Grace filled with gratitude.*

4. After the three-month arrangement for this condo and no recovery of our beach condo in sight, we then considered the purchase of the neighbor's condo, which could be accomplished with a reasonable interest payment. Jim balked at the idea since we had already taken one loan for the beach condo. We agreed that if he were to stop at the required office, and if someone was actually there (often not), and if it could be easily negotiated, then we would accept this next act of grace for supporting us through all the dislocation. Jim stopped. The negotiating loan officer who knew us was on hand. Jim returned with the signed papers, and we proceeded to the purchase. Grace abounded.

5. Next, there was a month that was not covered due to the owners being there a month longer than we needed. We were guided to a unit in the older neighboring condo. We cleaned it up and made do. We were again grateful for help.

6. We had stored all of our furniture and were equipped to move in. At the time of our sale of the Sea Chase Condo, we had really hoped to sell all of our furniture with it, but that was not the buyer's desire. So we had stored it all safely inland from Ivan and now had furniture available for our next move. We again felt blessed and provided for with the provision of this transaction.

7. Within a couple of months after moving in we were informed that once again property values were going up. The value of the condo unit we had just bought went up $125,000. We were awestruck. We also learned that home insurance would not be available due to the mass destruction of housing in the area.

8. By this time Jim's anxiety level was escalating as I related some increased costs with the home plans. He had asked me to take the lead on creating the house plans, as he could never figure them out on a flat piece of paper. Apparently, as I was quoting the rising cost of the plans, he was expressing distress with his friends on the courts. It was time for some honest consultation, and we began to weigh the values literally and figuratively.

    We now owned three properties: the 600+ square foot beach condo, this newly built and acquired Peninsula condo, and a large prime lot on the golf course with lakefront and some bay view. Our discussion centered around the property value that we held and the question: *If strong hurricanes and storms frequent this area and move the beach inland, is it wise to remain here?* We had one property on the beach and another a mile away that we were developing plans for. We lived in the third one adjacent to where the lot was located. Additional storms were already visiting the neighboring Florida shores. This was before Hurricane Katrina, which would arrive later that year. Jim was definitely fearful, and I was willing to move forward on an altered plan to sell the two Peninsula properties, move to Birmingham, and save the option to spend winters at the beach.

Birmingham was becoming enjoyable and attractive to us. The last few years in Alabama, we had traveled frequently to Birmingham to learn an allergy elimination technique and stayed with our MSIA extended family, Miller and Joy with their four children, where we received loving support and fellowship and held seminars together. We had been introduced the TND when Joy had asked for help to pick up the kids at the Montessori school at Mt Laurel where they attended. We were struck with the natural beauty of the area, the European-like atmosphere of the small town neighborhood, and the adjacent organic farm one mile down the road. We had been drawn to some type of sustainable living arrangement at some point in our lives as we began our golden years, and this looked like an answer to that vision. Now was as good a time as any.

9. One of Jim's tennis buddies, also a military retiree, was interested in the property at the Peninsula Golf and Racquet Club. Jim offered it at a fifty grand discount from our listing price, and the buyer in turn began to push for a further reduction. Jim, fearful under these pressing circumstances, was willing. I was not. I had already heard about the value of this property, and at the same time a leading magazine listing the top hundred places to retire had included the Peninsula Club in Gulf Shores. I

continued my research on the value of the property with
what was still available on their premises. I concluded
that our lot was the best buy at any comparable cost. I
asked Jim if I could present this argument and handle the
negotiation. He had provided so much for us and for me
over the years, and I wanted to do this for us with all of
my gratitude. He consented. I engaged with the friend
and then with his contractor, who was his brother with
a big, successful reputation. I wrote up and presented my
list of reasons for knowing the value of this lot, all of the
qualities of being there, the prime locale of the property,
and the fact that as soon as they had built, I was sure
that they knew they would be holding a million dollar
investment. I wanted it to be a win–win for them and
for us. Jim had initiated this negotiation with a fifty-
thousand-dollar friendship benefit, and if they were to
pass on the remaining value of the lot, we would restore
the initial price with the local Realtor the following day.
He complimented me on my research and said he would
move in our direction and meet us at the title company
the following day. Jim expected there would be further
negotiating conversation when we arrived. There was
none. It was complete. The same abundance also followed
us in the sale of the now existing condo we were living
in. Blessing after blessing followed us. We gave gratitude
and tithed to the source of our spiritual support with Joy
for the Grace and loving care for Jim and myself.

10. We ended up in Birmingham for our usual class with our
MSIA family and friends on Jim's birthday in April 2005.
I asked him what he would like to do for his celebration
day. He said, "Let's go back up to Mt Laurel and see
what is happening up there." We hadn't visited for several
months, and so we showed up. Della, who remains a dear
friend to this day at Mt Laurel, also the sales manager who

greeted us, escorted us from house to house with her golf cart. There were many new homes that we hadn't seen. The building progress was amazing. Earlier, some of the homes, being very close to each other, had not suited our transition from a big gorgeous view of the Gulf Bay for the past ten years.

11. But now, as we walked into a large category home on the corner of Burnham and Abbott, with the park across the street and the mountaintop view in the back, we ambled through the premises and then asked each other, "Do you like it?" We both nodded. Kenny, the contractor, was busy receiving some huge boxes of appliances. I could see an enclosed box with a refrigerator in it. We introduced ourselves, and as I said earlier, Jim and I had already chosen all the appliances we wanted in our next home, and we saw that we could now include some of them in this new home. So we announced to him, "Kenny, we want to buy this home, and we know that we don't want this refrigerator. Please don't open this box until we know if we can be here." He grinned. "Yes, ma'am," he said. He gathered his men, and they departed. We proceeded with our negotiations and the plans we would like added to this home. We were told that they had not worked with anyone who knew so well what they wanted. We knew them well. I had given up our former vision and plans, crying for a day with the loss of that joy, and then we moved on. We found comfort and joy as we took part in creating this smaller, lovely home with the inclusion of some of our original plans. We wanted also to be as green and nontoxic as possible and pulled out the gas range and the jet tubs for a safer stovetop and the new sanitary bubble tub. We chose safe, nontoxic wall paint and wood sealer without the toxic outgassing. The upper bedroom floors were covered with natural wool carpeting, and we

added some lovely wood cabinetry in place of the all-white fixtures throughout the premises. The wood and stone coordination on the main floor kitchen and living area was beautifully done, and again we felt gifted with the loving presence of Kenny and his crew who carried through on our ideas and allowed us a role in designing this next home to care for ourselves. It was the beginning of the next chapter of our lives together.

Creating and engaging with our new surroundings was our next adventure. Although resources and contacts were referred to us for tennis, a new ballroom studio existed in our neighborhood, and the weekly neighborhood Sippin' Seniors coffee time to get acquainted greeted us, Jim seemed to be more reclusive than he'd been in Gulf Shores with his longtime friends. Connecting with tennis players was more cumbersome. It involved making contact and then getting invited to groups already formed. And although we had started our ballroom dance classes in Gulf Shores, he was reluctant to start here at the nearby studio in the Mt Laurel village.

I had solicited Jim for this weekly activity a few months earlier when I had learned, from a posted research article, that ballroom dancing was the number one exercise for the prevention and reversal of dementia and Alzheimer's. A well-researched article was posted at the new local senior center in Gulf Shores, and classes were offered by a couple for the winter months. Our new Orange Beach health club in our community was also offering classes. Jim was sure that it was not for him, but I asked him to remember when I really did not want to learn tennis and how I was encouraged so strongly on my ability. I said it was something very important for me—and for us, since my mother now had dementia and his mother was being cared for in an Alzheimer's program. I wanted us to have this weekly date time for some mutual interest and nurturing for our relationship. I said that I would visit first and check it out. After attending the class at the health club, I told the young instructor of Jim's hesitance due to his dyslexia and some issues of coordination. Jim always spoke of sensing that the top of his body did not always seem coordinate with his lower body. It was an understandable concern.

The instructor was very attentive to my inquiries and Jim's concerns and then brought over his younger brother, who was assisting, and said that he was also very dyslexic and had found that learning to dance was very helpful. As I explained this to Jim, he consented with the awareness that the nurturing time would be good for us. As for me, dancing was always something that I wanted more of. So we got started with the group meetings, and before long he announced that if we were going to do this, then we should purchase a package and meet privately for some lessons. We were signed up and had three lessons when Hurricane Ivan passed through. Afterwards the dance studio was in total disarray and was henceforth out of business.

We'd lost a few hundred dollars on the adventure, and now Jim was not interested in the venue at hand in Mt Laurel. He spent a great deal of time with the mathematical numbers he loved and time in his new office on the second floor of our home and worked on the investment tracking of all of the trusts he cared for with his family. His new dance centered around numbers. He became attracted to the game of Sudoku. He was, in fact, mesmerized with it and advanced to a Master's Level with this game. I joined for some beginner level play, and even at bedtime he and I would work on a game before sleep. We played Sudoku, said our prayers, called in the Light, and set Intention for our evening travels with our Soul Transcendence to finish our day.

He did play some tennis matches on a weekly basis and made it often to the courts in the neighboring city of Pelham, where many of the Alabama State Finals for the USTA tennis leagues were held. There were twenty-five or thirty beautiful clay courts and some cement courts as well, where the local schools brought their students. I got involved with the women's senior USTA teams and found a lovely group of women and new friendships. The men however, did not have any competitive teams with the USTA sections, and Jim was resolved to play when invited for leisure. Jim enjoyed the play, but the competitive edge to escalate his game was missing.

Our second spring at Mt Laurel, in 2007, brought with it a southern drought. The abundance of trees that made the area so beautiful also released a great deal of pollen. The extensive spring release of pollen created allergic reactions for all of us. We sneezed and coughed and took whatever was recommended—lots of vitamin C drinks and cough lozenges with horehound (for blood type B)—and through it all Jim played tennis every chance he got. He had played the year following Hurricane Ivan on the beach with the eruption of molds, and now here throughout the drought with the excessive pollen. He assured me that when he was playing, he did not cough, and as always he came home to talk of his game of the day.

But his cough continued. I would even go out in the morning before he left and hose off the inch of pollen that covered the ground and our porch to make a path to Jim's Toyota Sequoia so he could leave for the courts. Eventually some rain appeared, and throughout the neighborhood our coughing ceased. Jim's cough did not. He continued and still assured me that during play on the courts he was not coughing. That week I happened on the court next to him while taking a clinic session with friends and heard his persistent coughing. Ann, our tennis professional for the clinic, asked if Jim was okay. She had noticed his cough before today, since his game was often on the court next to her. I had been unaware that his cough was so persistent, and on this day he stopped early due to his discomfort. I approached him with my concern and declared that we would get to the doctor today. We did.

Our doctor immediately took x-rays and then put them up for us to see them. She declared that it was the worst case of walking pneumonia she had ever seen and gave us some antibiotic with the instruction that if he was not well in ten days, we would do an MRI. I couldn't help asking myself, *What would that be for?* The cough persisted. We returned for the MRI on a Friday. On Monday he returned to Dr. Law for the results. She was very upset that I wasn't with him, as we had guests. Jim came home and said that the exams were worse. He showed me the results, indicating some possible allergic involvement or some kind of cancer. I was sure it was the allergy that we had treated over and over for so many years. He did not tell me that he was referred to an oncologist but said he wanted to pursue an alternative care program that his acupuncturist had told him about in Tijuana, Mexico. The doctor wanted to do a biopsy here, and he had understood from his doctor friend that it was not advised to disturb the possible cancer cells with this method. We immediately made arrangements for the Oasis of Hope in Tijuana, Mexico, where it became necessary to do the biopsy. The results showed us that within the ten days that it took to get there, the growth in his lungs had doubled in size, and the challenge lay before us for success of treatment.

We learned about their protocol that was researched and initiated by Dr. Francisco Contreras with his book called *Dismantling Cancer*. We began their IV protocol immediately. Follow-up x-rays told us that the cancer had stopped all growth! Immediately, with the first week's protocol all growth had ceased. It was encouraging to see, but now he would need to reverse the damage already done in his lungs, where the rapid growth had consumed nearly half of his lung capacity. Jim received the natural chemotherapy with open arms and with gratitude to all of the wonderful staff, the simple and sterile environment, including my rooming with him in our private space, and all of the amenities included in this holistic approach. We met with our social worker, were invited to the daily spiritual support, and learned of the dining facilities for both of us, which included an

CHAPTER 23

Seeing and Knowing His Time of Passing

The last morning of our final visit to the Oasis of Hope in Tijuana, Jim awakened early, and I adjusted his bed for him for comfort to breathe. It was too early to rise, and we agreed to do some SEs (Spiritual Exercises/ meditation) before getting ready to depart. We settled in and called ourselves into the Light. I fell back into sleep, and a very vivid dream appeared.

Jim awoke with joy, and I was in tears. He wanted me to know, "I just had the greatest dream!" he said. "I was going down this beautiful road, and I made it to the end! It was beautiful and so light-filled, and I made it to the end of the road!" he said over and over as he got out of bed.

After I had listened intently, I related my dream: "My dear friend Carol was with me in my dream." (Carol's husband had died the year before with cancer). "We were both curled up on the ground and crying. We cried and cried. I knew we were crying for the loss of her husband, Bob, but I didn't know why I was crying. We were just both crying together." But I did hear and know what might be happening when I heard Jim's dream and his joy at the clarity of his vision. He had made it to the end of the road. He had accomplished what was important to him, and he had made it to the end of the road for this lifetime. I felt it in my heart and in my knowing.

He had already told me how he had resolved all his debt, which was a lifetime direction for him financially. He had managed the trust funds for his children and turned them over to them. We had been through years of transition after his thirty-three years of teaching and ten years of beautiful beach and hurricanes. Through all our trials, he played tennis in Michigan and in both our homes in Alabama. He had studied and practiced Soul Transcendence for years in the company of others in the Movement of Spiritual Inner Awareness (MSIA) and knew his way home to God within. He found the perfect game of numbers to appease his process and played Sudoku to the maximum level. He was already at Master level, figuring numbers in the winning order with nearly no numbers to go on. To watch him was beyond my comprehension. But he seemed to know.

And now he knew that he had made it to the end of the road. I heard it and knew. We were not coming back to the Oasis. We would do whatever was next, as he might see it. He still talked of making a showing at the senior doubles finals for USTA. He spoke of it to his friends and family. He would tell us, "I'm going to get well and make it to the seventies and over National Championships."

This was after the third month of care at the Oasis of Hope. His loss of strength would not allow us to return, and we engaged a local oncologist who was our neighbor in Mt Laurel to administer the American protocol of chemotherapy. She wanted an aggressive approach with a daily gentle amount of chemo for the cancer that remained in his lung; she also noted that the small nodule of cancer in his liver was not growing and would be closely monitored. The cancer did not abate, and the growth reengaged. He did the radiation therapy on the esophagus, and the tumor was eliminated, and a feeding tube was inserted in an artery in his arm. We were not informed that the side effects of the radiation would or could alleviate the message to his brain to eat. He could *not* eat! The tumor was gone with the radiation treatment, but he could not eat! The message to his brain and body was that he was *full*! After three bites of food, he begged to know if he could take another bite when I sat a small plate in front of him. I was saddened to see the pain of his loss of nourishment and joy with eating. Soon the IV feeding did not integrate into his circulation for strength or nourishment. The solution pooled in his body and was no longer feeding him. It was a useless effort on his part! His body no longer worked as designed.

The tube feeding was discontinued when the doctor came by the house to see Jim. Interestingly the day before we had gotten the lab results for his liver function that was again reported normal. That next day she came by with the x-rays that showed the growth of the tumor in his liver. There would be no more chemo; it had been distressing to his system. The primary disturbance for Jim, other than the lethargy, was that his focus and ability to do his SEs—prayer and meditation time—had disappeared. His sense of being with God in his Spiritual Exercising time as he had known it and experienced it was gone. "Where is it?" he would say. "I don't like this feeling."

His maintenance at this time was through the abundance of people who in many ways let him know of their prayers and Light being sent his way. He received a prayer shawl, a new Bible edition, books of encouragement, notes, and cards, and neighbors showed up to do yard work or water my flowers or tell us they had his name on their mirror for morning prayers to God. We read daily e-mails from John-Roger from his devotional, at Loving Each Day.org. These seemed so often to be written just for Jim and me, and we lifted into the Light with gratitude for all of these gifts. They were incredibly sustaining.

In fact, abundant and amazing evidence of the sustaining nature of God's loving came through the caring assistance offered to us by friends and neighbors in Mt Laurel. As we moved home for constant care, Jim needed help during the night. He could no longer go up and down stairs to our bedroom and slept in a bed we made for him downstairs in the living room. But he often got up for the bathroom and needed assistance. A couple of the neighborhood men volunteered. Then a lovely woman who did this service came and watched Jim all evening. But as we utilized these services, Jim became more and more uncomfortable with them. We had gotten hospice services and coaching for these home services, but to have someone watching him all night in our home was uncomfortable. He said that the last lady never took her eyes off him, and it made him uncomfortable. He asked me, "Could we please work something out without them?"

"Okay," I said. "Let's see how it could work. Let's ask how God would guide us through this." So we called in the Light of God. "Dear God, we call ourselves forward into Your Light. We ask for the presence of the Christ and the Holy Spirit to fill, surround, and protect us and lead us in the way that would be of Divine Loving service for Jim and myself. I need sleep, Lord, and Jim needs help when he gets up. We ask for your presence of perfect care from you." *And so it happened.*

I would awaken and go downstairs just as Jim needed me. I tucked him back into bed with kisses and massage to his back for comfort, and I returned upstairs and returned to sleep. Again around 4:30 a.m., I would awaken and go to him as he was awakening and needed care. The synchrony was awesome and beloved. We felt the embrace of God's divine and loving service with us. It just kept happening this way. We had these daily and nightly times of offering our trust and faith with God and however it was to be. Just now it makes me cry and laugh at the same time with the precious presence of it.

The greatest Presence of God was with us and provided perfectly.

Twelve days after the report that the cancer had enlarged in Jim's liver and there was no more care that could be done, Jim declared that he wanted his family with him. "Where are they? Why aren't they here?" He had said he wanted them to be here for Thanksgiving, and this was the week before. I immediately called them, and they all got their flights arranged, including his sister Cleora in California, his son and daughter-in-law and grandson, Troy, Krista, and Collin in Arizona, were on their way. His daughter and her fiancé, Carrie and Chris, came from Colorado, and his first daughter and three of the granddaughters, Claire, Stephanie, Jacqueline, and Audrey, came from Seattle. His niece and her husband, Sherri and Kevin, with their son, Andrew, came from Austin, Texas. His nephew and family, Travis, Dawn, Alex, and Ashton, arrived from Michigan. They all arrived in the next few days.

On the eighteenth day after the discontinuation of therapy we all surrounded Jim as he rested peacefully with all the adult family members and our friends, Miller and Joy, who joined our ministry with the rest of the family. We were playing the recording of the Prayer of Love so beautifully given to us from John-Roger followed by the Ani Hu chant for the alignment and attunement with the inner presence with God. We held the Light into the room with Jim from that Inner Source within each of us.

I had left the area to attend to a needed function upstairs when Jim's niece Sherri came to get me. Kevin had sent her when he felt and heard Jim's breathing change. I came to return to his side; his sister, Cleora, sat at one side and I at his other. Jim had asked me before, when we talked about his departure, "What shall I do? What will it be like?"

I had responded, "Just breathe into God, honey. Your breath will be waiting for you. Just take your breath into God."

So now was that time. His breaths became fewer and shorter, and finally, after a delay came the last breath. As this breath left, the *Light*, this beautiful presence of the *Light of God*, fell upon Jim.

It was a palpable presence for me as I participated in it. It was a fullness in the room, and we all had our experience with it and the sound of God with the chanting of the Ani Hu. We sat in silence and tears as we took it in. The Joy of the Light enfolded me, and I knew through my tears that there was Joy with Jim's freedom from the body that no longer was working for him. His new body of Light had consumed him, and he passed from us to his new place of eternal existence.

CHAPTER 24

A New View!

This time, a great personal loss was a very different experience than with Emily. My grieving as I had known of it with Emily was now turned into the great healer of the divine *Joy* expressed fully in this moment and my forthcoming days. I knew of it. I had practiced it with Jim, and he with me, as we had studied through all these years of healing and knowing that eternal life is real, just as Emily had guided me to ask, listen, and receive. Following all the years of learning and knowing her presence on the other side, it was now my experience to know Jim's passing into this glorious presence of Light here with us. He had completed his physical life here, and I was to stay as a witness of it and the knower of the eternal *Joy*—a joy that extends beyond the words of my experience. The experience of Heaven on Earth was now that gift given by this experience with Jim's passing.

Troy and Krista arrived shortly thereafter with their son, Collin James Daily, Jim's namesake grandson. He had landed at the Birmingham airport as Jim passed and came to settle into our experience as we shared it with them. The children came in from outside, said their good-byes to Grandy, shed their tears, and sat with all of us as we held each other in hugs.

But we didn't stop there. Troy, who was now a graduated

chef, began Thanksgiving dinner in honor of his dad. We played videos that Cleora had brought of all of the years they had been together, we told stories, and the many Sudoku books that lay around were distributed. We ate, and we celebrated the year and day of Jim's passing into his eternal existence with the divine heritage of God for each of us.

We spent the next couple of days together. When Jim's family departed, some of my family arrived to be with me for the next week. The story was alive and well within me. I had received the greatest of blessings for my life. I had begged God to let me know where my daughter was when I could no longer be with her and care for her. I had been brought to this blessed man, James Thornton Daily, who was my partner for nearly twenty years, to find that awareness of the greatest church within me for God's inner presence through a gathering of people who called themselves the Movement of Spiritual Inner Awareness. It is that church that we all know of no matter where we find to worship nor where we may find ourselves on the path of knowing Love and the inner Presence of Spirit. I found and know of not only the existence of God's plan within me but also the awareness of the eternal path that we are all on, as shown to me with the experiences with these two people and all those who showed up in between for my learning and support throughout the years. I had passed from a life of grieving, as a victim of pain, to Joy and eternal knowing and experiencing of Love that has gone way beyond my asking and greater than I can even know today. I keep on this journey of Loving and learning as I continue.

CHAPTER 25

Grand Memorials

We held a memorial service for Jim with our dear neighbors and friends in our community of Mt Laurel, who planted a tree in his memory in the corner of our yard. It grows with great strength. We had a service with his comrades of the tennis courts in Gulf Shores and then again in Kalamazoo, Michigan, where he spent his years of teaching and early growth. Friends from all times of his life, including his years at Howe Military Academy, showed up. But more than this, his students from thirty-three years began to send messages, many from across the nation and around the world. They wrote what Mr. D had meant to them on the website for his obituary. They were messages that profoundly acknowledged how their self-image had expanded and grown and how the lessons and skills they'd learned from Mr. D were forever in their lives!

What follows is my record of his memorial service as it was delivered to the group of friends and family that gathered.

Birthing into Spirit with James T. Daily

Memorial Service

Our beloved minister Jim Daily passed into Spirit on November 17, 2007, at 4:20 p.m. with his family surrounding him and the sounds of chanting from Our Song of Love. The Light was full and embracing us all as he took his last breath and quietly, peacefully completed this lifetime and returned home.

It had been six months since we heard of the diagnosis of esophageal cancer, and only then because, as this cancer makes itself known, it had metastasized into the lungs and slightly into the liver. We pursued holistic services at the Oasis of Hope hospital in Tijuana, Mexico. The treatment and care were superb, with natural substances that immediately halted all growth in the lungs and offered all organic foods and wonderful educational support along the way for us to understand all the services for physical, mental, emotional, and spiritual support and healing. Jim was trusting and visualized how he would find wellness in his choices and win the seventies and older tennis doubles championship in the years to come. He wanted to see his grandchildren grow and continue our lives together in our ministries.

As we embraced the whole treatment regimen, ate all the right foods for alkalizing the body, and welcomed family and friends to our home for support and care, we tuned in to how we heard the Light working for us.

We ended most evenings by acknowledging how this day had worked for us and gave gratitude. Jim would say, "This was a *good* day." We knew that *good* was just the long form for *God*, and we thanked God each day for the creators we could be in it. We would read from the e-mails and cards that had arrived that day or from a devotional book someone had sent, but mostly we listened to the quotes from Loving Each Day (LED). There were days when I knew that J-R and John were surely sending them just for us and for Jim.

This was one of the earlier quotes (from John Morton) that came to us:

> Educate yourself on your conditions and look for simple measures that can contribute to improving your health and vitality. Remember that your state of mind, the way you feel about yourself, powerfully contributes or not to your well being depending on whether your attitude is uplifting or not. God is alive and well within you, waiting in a moment's notice your call for assistance on all levels. Use your creatorship wisely to direct what you need while being trusting that there is a good purpose in every condition in which you are dealing.

We continued on, and as Jim weakened and we could no longer make the trips to Mexico for the superb treatment there, we continued with our neighbor oncologist, who would maintain a protocol for us and would be nearby. Jim continued to say that he would show up on the courts when he'd passed through this time, and he felt safe and secure with each decision as we participated with new loving people at our neighborhood service. At each step, grace and ease were provided as found ways to serve Jim as he was able to care for himself and with assistance as needed. We were grateful for all the prayers, abundance of Light extended, and seeds that were shared through many in the MSIA community.

Then came a next LED after many others that we gained strength from (this one from John-Roger). Jim responded with, "Read that again!" So I read again:

> It seems like there are more terrible things occurring on this planet than there has ever been before. We have had 2000 years of the Christ energy, influence and information,

and there are all these terrible things happening. Is being Christian a failure? Some people might look at it in that way, but let's look at another point of view.

Have you ever taken a bucket that's been sitting outside, turned on the hose to fill it with water, and had the water gush out of the hose really fast and, as it hits the bucket, all the dirt and debris that's in the bottom shoots up and gets all over you? You jump back and say, "Oh, my God, I've got junk all over me!" And it looks like there's more junk on you than there ever could have been in the bottom of that bucket.

What we are seeing on the planet right now appears to be more junk than ever could have been in the bottom of the bucket. That's because Spirit is being shot into an area that is bringing it all up. The action of Spirit is bringing up all the junk and crud that's been sitting in the bottom of that bucket for centuries. It's being brought up to be dealt with.

How do you deal with it? Skim it off. Then you put more water in the bottom of the bucket; you fill it until the junk floats up to the surface and falls away, and then the water flows up naturally clean and pure.

Sending the Light for the Highest Good often and neutrally helps the bucket get clean. We can apply this analogy to some of the global situations that exist in our world right now. You can also apply it to things that happen in your own life.

Jim and I began to talk about the fact that he had not fought in a war in this lifetime. He had grown up in military school, but he had committed to being a Spiritual Warrior, and clearly what was coming to him was his war and service as a spiritual warrior. He was serving more than himself, and he had chosen perfectly for his purpose at this time. He embraced this idea with tears and appreciation of the acknowledgment of his process. He was awestruck with the amount of Loving that continued to visit him, and this was one of those moments of awareness.

As it came clearer that this treatment protocol was not creating his intended outcome, there were more messages. Jim learned on October 31 that the treatments were not containing or reversing the disease, and we received this LED message from John-Roger:

> I made a spiritual promise to the people I work with in Spirit, and every one of you know that I have kept my word with you, even when you broke yours. I kept mine, and even when you break yours tomorrow, I will keep mine, because I didn't say that I would do it if you did what I told you to do. I said, "Yes, I'll work with you … unconditionally." That eliminates chaos in God. It brings direction, it brings completion, it brings the ability to endure all things. Jesus, the Master said, "He wins who endures to the end," but not in those words.

Jim's passing was eighteen days after the news of October 31. All of his family surrounded him. The children were outside and were called into the house to witness Grandy and his passing. We cried, we held each other in silence, and we prayed for Jim and his soul as the Light of his passing permeated our place of his departure. Two of the granddaughters were on my lap next to the bed. With tears, Jackie said, "But Nanny, this is my birthday!"

And in that moment I offered, "But Jackie, Grandy chose your birthday to have the biggest birthday ever! He chose your birthday to birth home to God! This is the biggest birthday we all get to have! We have our first birthday when we come into these bodies; we have a lot that we need to do here and then we get to go home to God where Grandy gets to be free from the cancer and be his wonderful happy self!"

Jackie got it! She started describing all of the wonderful things

she could see Grandy doing. She began laughing, and we all felt
the joy of Jim's spirit, we laughed with her and with the joy of
Spirit that surrounded us, and we began to celebrate the Greatest
Birthday! Later that day Jackie added a candle to her birthday cake
for Grandy to further acknowledge his special day with her. We
all sang joyfully for both of them. We celebrated the rest of that
day and the next just as he had wanted with Thanksgiving for
all of us and all of the loving Jim had brought into our lives: we
looked at pictures and remembered *when*, we watched childhood
movies that had been put onto DVD by Jim's sister, and we played
some Sudoku just to keep up with some of the numbers Jim had
shared with us all his adult life. The kids talked about Grandy with
some endearing stories, the nieces and nephews talked of Uncle
Jim, Cleora held her brother near all her life as was displayed in
the movies, his kids talked about Dad, and I shared about my
wonderful husband and his courage throughout his years with the
challenges his body came with. Even students from all of the years
of math classes that Jim taught for thirty-three years sent messages
of what they learned from Mr. D and how he still impacted their
lives now. It was a majestic memorial and celebration!

As we had proceeded during his care, I'd learned that the
more I engaged in just holding my loving service for Jim and
with Jim, the greater were the strength and endurance available
to me in more ways than I knew how to measure. For that great
learning I am grateful, and I continue to know and experience the
Light that lifted Jim in his resurrection, just as I continue to follow
the loving into my day today. I found the strength of loving for
Jim and with Jim, and I choose to go on as I celebrate the Light
presence and the resurrection in me with the greatness of that
lesson of Loving. "There is really no presence of sorrow or grief,
just the loving and joy," I tell others as they express their sorrow
for my loss. I say, "it really isn't there. There is only the joy of his
departure into God's great Light and the courage and loving that

we shared!" There really is only change, and I already know how to follow the Light that was our constant partner.

Years ago, after the sudden passing of my eleven-year-old daughter and a great deal of pain and grief, I asked God how to get to Heaven Within, and I was led to Insight, MSIA, and then to USM for a few years and all of the wonderful and practical teachings of John-Roger and then John Morton into my Soul awareness. I have been prepared in amazing ways! And in every way I am grateful. Now I attend the doctoral program with the Peace Theological Seminary to become my own Spiritual Scientist! What more could I ask for? More, that's all. There will always be more.

A next LED that arrived that I found was the truth in me reads, *"In love we bring forward all things, in love we maintain all things, and in love we change all things."*

I thank you, my Beloved John-Roger, for all the teachings as Jesus brought them to us. Thank you, John Morton, for all you share with the abundance of blessings and your support for all that is and will be ….

Thank you, Jim, for being a Love Teacher these wonderful twenty years. My gratitude is full.

Your beloved, Judith M. Daily

After his 'professional' tennis play of the day!

His fellow professionals headed for the next championship

PART FIVE

PERSONAL HISTORY

CHAPTER 26

My Lifetime

Judith Marie, *born* October 10, 1944; *birthed* Emily Janel: June 1, 1972.

I was born and raised in Kalamazoo, Michigan. During my early childhood it was just Mom (born Joyce Margaret Harmon) and me, while Dad; Samuel Gruizenga, made his way through the shores of Normandy and into Europe; a soldier fighting in World War II. Just as the song "I've Got a Gal in Kalamazoo" was making headlines, I turned thirteen months, and Dad made his way home to his two gals in Kalamazoo. I took my very first steps with arms opened wide to greet him. My brother, Ted Merle, arrived seven months later following Dad's homecoming. Seven years later my sister Pamela Joyce was born. My brother and I adored being big brother and sister to help care for her.

Dad's mother and father emigrated from the Netherlands. Samuel was next to the youngest of fourteen children. He grew up with the remaining eight brothers and two sisters after the passing of three siblings at a young age. They all grew up and had families and lived in or near the Kalamazoo area. Our primary socialization and weekend entertainment included visiting with each other in our homes where thirty of us cousins enjoyed the gatherings. Most of the family attended the Reformed or Christian

Reformed Church of America, along with many neighbors who were also of Dutch lineage.

Dad was a brilliant young man with great abilities for learning. His education was disrupted during high school when the family's home burned down. Sam dropped out of high school to help rebuild the family home along with the other brothers. When he returned, his counselor told him he would never catch up with the rest of his class. With disregard and discouragement and Dutch stubborn nature, he joined the army and went to war with Germany. His formal education ended.

My father was gifted with a photographic memory and a natural ability to memorize and learn foreign languages. In school he had loved history, could recall whole textbook passages, and aced his class studies. In the service, his superior officers quickly realized these skills would be useful in Intelligence. He was assigned to a team whose work was to anticipate the enemy's movements to gain tactical advantages for the Americans.

My father never spoke of his war experiences. When he finally did, it was 1963, and I was in college. I came home to tell him that my boyfriend and I had left campus to see the movie *The Longest Day,* about the invasion of Normandy. As I spoke of how the movie started and what was happening, *he* finished the movie for me just as I had seen it. I was shocked that he knew so much about it.

He was there. He had participated fully in what I had just seen on the screen. What he shared is deeply imprinted in my mind. His best friend from home was shot and died next to him. He was in the third wave of the invasion that finally broke through the German defenses. The sadness and devastating loss he experienced was accompanied with the pride of being a part of the force that liberated the Netherlands, where his parents were born.

After returning from the war, my father wasn't an easy man to live with. Although we knew he loved us deeply, his flashes of pain and anger were a continual prevailing characteristic that we all had to learn to live with. My brother Ted resisted and was often the object of my father's brutality. I was deeply affected by my father's hurtful behavior toward him and my mother as well. I took on the job of family counselor at an early age and tried to deflect or run interference as I anticipated Dad's moods.

I was five years old when we moved to our first home on the north side of Kalamazoo, one block from the parents of Dad's best friend who did not come home. Another side to Dad came out as he made frequent visits to them, with Teddy and me in tow.

I attended the local elementary with our neighborhood gang of thirty kids and then junior high school east of our home neighborhood and did well. In high school, my classes were more challenging, and my first laborious assignment to write a term paper was deemed a failure. I had never received a grade lower than a C until then, and our English instructor assured most of us in the classroom that we were inept. Many parents showed up in the hallway the next morning to protest, but not mine. From then on and into college, I was convinced of my inability to write and avoided all classes and professors who required writing projects. The thought never occurred to me that I would someday write a story in the form of a memoir that others could read.

My high school counselor announced to my parents and myself that I wouldn't make it through college. I proved him wrong. Then I went on to two nursing programs: the first was in psychiatry as a psychiatric attendant nurse and the second was an associate degree in science to complete my state board exams to become a registered nurse.

After completing my year at Western Michigan for some basic classes, I moved from home with two friends to attend a psychiatric attendant nursing program at Pine Rest Christian Hospital, a large psychiatric facility in a nearby city which was supported by our church. We had a year of amazing and interesting class curriculum and fulfilling dormitory life.

After graduating and becoming licensed, I began working

at Pine Rest. I worked initially with teenagers and then with chronically ill women who were long-term residents. Many were receiving electroshock therapy and heavy drugs. With many clients we saw the reversal of dysfunctional symptoms and helped foster and support meaningful living skills with innovative approaches. Eventually, most clients graduated into community housing with employment abilities. It was my privilege to have participated in this progressive team process.

Then after working at Pine Rest for a year, I was offered scholarship funding to attend a community college to work toward an associate degree in science to become a registered nurse. After completing the program, I moved into nursing supervision at Pine Rest. There were multiple services at this facility, including services for special needs children with variations of mental disabilities and for chronic and long-term clients with schizophrenia, depression, and other long-term disorders, as well as acute care for those who needed therapy and stabilization from home stressors.

I learned and knew how to be with disturbed people and give them the professional care they needed for recovery. My experience also helped me see how to live with and love my father despite his disturbing behavior. Even though he would not agree to professional help, I knew he had prepared the way for me to wake up to this service.

I married in 1967, the year I graduated from Kellogg Community College. Five years later, after moving to Pasadena, California, I received the greatest gift of my life, the birth of my lovely and brilliant daughter, Emily Janel, in 1972. My first years of parenting led me to pursue a master's program in human development at Pacific Oaks College in Pasadena, California. My master's degree and project became the development of an infant toddler developmental program at our Presbyterian Church in Arcadia, California. Together, Emi and I grew up in our educational endeavors: she in her preschool and elementary classroom and I in my return to college once more to produce a master's thesis relative to this curriculum. It was a grueling endeavor for me, and during the course of it, my father passed, and then Emily followed three years later. I eventually sought private tutoring to complete my thesis.

When I was thirty-four years old, my father was diagnosed with lung cancer, which I assumed was the result of smoking Camel cigarettes from the time he was a young soldier. He finally quit when my sister Beth was born, and he and mom were forty-one and forty-two years of age. However, the damage to his lungs had already set in. He died during treatment when he hemorrhaged in the middle of the night from a simultaneous ulcerative condition. The doctor was *not* notified, and he passed in the morning. An autopsy showed that the cancer had actually subsided. His nightly Alka-Seltzer from chronic stomach distress resulted in this final bleeding ulcer.

Nine months after Dad passed, Mom was diagnosed with uterine cancer. The doctor related that the tumor had taken nine months to grow. My sister Beth was eleven years old at the time. Mom knew she needed to recover for herself and Beth. Because of the stress, Mom asked me to return to Kalamazoo from California for support. I had separated and divorced from Emily's father, and we willingly moved to Michigan to be with Mom and Beth. Mom worked with a new holistic health program at a local hospital and by the end of the year had reversed the condition. She even got into therapy for herself as a new single parent with lots of transitions and healing to do.

The four of us stayed together that year of chemotherapy, and Mom slowly recovered her strength. We praised God and celebrated with her for being such a courageous participant in her therapy. Mom religiously did her visualizations and meditation prayers. She was eating healthily, and we eliminated white foods and sugars and supplemented with what we knew at that time. After her diagnosis as cancer-free, we learned that Mom's was the most aggressive form of uterine cancer. We focused to support Beth to help her adjust to the passing of her daddy. We all attended church and sang together in the choir and at the piano when Mom would play for us. We played table games endlessly with Emily's perseverance and enjoyed our favorite family TV programs. We endeavored to lift ourselves and each other with hugs and new life with God's grace and help.

The trauma of Emily's sudden death in 1983 began my search to find her. As part of that experience, I eventually completed two master's degrees: one in spiritual psychology and the second in consciousness, health, and healing from the University of Santa Monica in California, with many requirements for writing from an inner presence of guidance. Through this process, writing became a new companion. From this reconnection, I regained trust in the validity of my own words and ability to express. From this joy and healing, I am grateful to share the process of these cherished pages of my life's journey.

== END MATTER ==

ENDNOTES

Songs of Comfort:

"Jesus Loves Me" Words by Anna B. Warner 1820–1915.
    Music by William B. Bradley 1816–1868.

"Away in a Manger"
    Words by (stanza 3) John Thomas McFarland 1851–1913.
    Music by James R. Murray 1841–1905

"Because He Lives"
    "Because I live, you also will live" John 14:19 NIV
    Words by Gloria Gaither
    Music by William J. Gaither, copyright 1971.

Biblical Scriptures taken from:

The Thompson Chain-Reference Bible, New International Version (NIV)

John 14:2–4: "In my Father's house are many rooms; if it were not so, I would have told you. I am going there to prepare a place for you. And if I go and prepare a place for you, I will come back and take you to be with me that you also may be where I am. You know the way to the place where I am going."

Matthew 7:8 "For everyone who asks, receives; he who seeks finds; and to him who knocks, the door will be opened."

The phrase: *"LET GO AND LET GOD"* --taken from compilation of texts:

Philippians 4:6–7; John 14:27; Matthew 11:28–30
Also, 1 Peter 5:7: "Cast all your anxiety on Him because He cares for you."

John 14:12: "I tell you the truth, anyone who has faith in me will do what I have been doing. He will do even greater things than these, because I am going to the Father.
Reworded by John-Roger, "This that I do you too shall do and even greater."

BIBLIOGRAPHY

1. Rogers, Catherine H., Frank J. Floyd, Marsha Mailick Seltzer, Jan Greenberg, and Jinkuk Hong. Long-term Effects of the Death of a Child on Parents' Adjustment in Midlife. *J. Fam Psychol.* 2008 Apr 22(2): 203–211.
   (Correspondence regarding this article, email: ffloyd@ gsu.edu).
2. Hendrix, Harville. *Getting the Love You Want.* New York: Henry Holt and Co., [date].
3. D'Adamo, Peter, with Catherine Whitney. *Eat Right for4 Your Type – 4 Blood Types, 4 Diets.* New York: G.P. Putnam's Sons, 1996.
4. D'Adamo, Peter, with Catherine Whitney. *Live Right for4 Your Type – 4 Blood Types, 4 Programs.* New York: G.P. Putnam's Sons, 2001.
5. D'Adamo, Peter, with Catherine Whitney. *Blood Type B or A or O or AB – Food, Beverage and Supplement Lists.* New York: Berkley, 2002.
6. John-Roger, D.S.S. *Fulfilling Your Spiritual Promise,* 3 volumes. Los Angeles: Mandeville Press, 2006. Guidelines of MSIA: pages 3–5, 655, 971, 1109. Spiritual Exercises: pages 395–453.
7. John-Roger. *Loving Each Day for Peacemakers – Choosing Peace Every Day.* Los Angeles: Mandeville Press, 2002. Daily

devotional sent from Loving-Each-Day.org from John-Roger and John Morton, Spiritual Director of the Movement of Spiritual Inner Awareness (MSIA).

8. John-Roger D.S.S. *The Wayshower: A Traveler Through the Ages.* Los Angeles: Mandeville Press, 1992.

REFERENCES

1. *Getting the Love You Want* Relationship Therapy. Information available at www.ImagoRelationships.org
2. Insight Educational Seminars. Contact www.InsightSeminars.org or www.Insightoneworld.org. Call 1-800-311-8001. Joey Hubbard, President/CEO.
3. University of Santa Monica, Spiritual Psychology with Drs. Ron and Mary Hulnick. Programs offered for Soul-Centered Living. Call 310-829-7402. Address: 2107 Wilshire Boulevard, Santa Monica, California. www.universityofSantaMonica.edu
4. Movement of Spiritual Inner Awareness. Full contact information, references, live webcasts, literature available at www.msia.org. Call 323-737-4055.
   The Journey of a Soul by John-Roger, free book upon request.
5. Peace Theological Seminary and College of Philosophy. www.pts.org

APPENDIX

I am writing to share with you some of my news about my daughter, Emily's death and to request your support and assistance. The time is at hand to make some public comments and recommendations to infuence the legislative activity with the newly proposed State Regulations for Camps in Michigan.

The autopsy and pathology reports portray that Emily's body was perfectly healthy with the exception of a small heart anomaly that **can** develop into difficulties in later life. Emily's heart tissue did not show any unhealthy conditions from this heart anomaly. It is also undetectable in early life. Athletes in college and professional play who have died suddenly have also been known to have this anomaly with varied opinions of its effect on death. Because of Emily's ill symptoms prior to her death and her continuation of strenuous play and the history of Emily having had a prior episode of a heart block during severe illness, the pathologist believes that the combination was the cause of her death.

My concern is about the absence of appropriate assessment of Emily's prior symptoms, inadequate diagnosis and treatment of those symptoms, the neglect of the doctor nor family being notified even though her ill symptoms persisted beyond 24-36 hours. Those decisions were then made without a physical or adequate history for making appropriate judgments by the health official. I am concerned about the manner in which she was listened to or lack of it, even though she returned for help several times as well as the lack of knowledge of normal growth and development to make decisions for the limited abilities of the preadolescent to make their own health decisions coupled with the vulnerabilities of their rapidly growing bodies.

Camp is a beneficial experience for children, but it is not the ultimate experience of a child's life. A child should not be expected to make-it or tough-it-out to get through a week of camp experience if that experience becomes painful because of physical illness or inability to make contact with one's family for comfort, support or help. It is all too common that camps, in fact, discourage contacts with families through nonavailability of the use of a phone and discouraging receiving of letters from home by imposing intimidating jokes upon those who do.

I believe that the above concerns represent a violation of family and children's rights; for parents to make the health care decisions about their child and for children to be able to ask for support or help from their parents.

I am therefore requesting your support to make the following recommendations to be incorporated in the new State Regulations and Guidelines. Please support these issues by placing a check in the box preceeding each recommendation and place your signature with any comment or opinion at the bottom of the form. The form is written in the requested format for public hearing discussion according to the numbered categories for the proposed rules of public act no. 116, 1973. The timeline for receiving these recommendations is Friday, December 9, but after meeting with legislative representative Mary Brown and she, in turn, contacting David G. Fitzgerald of D.S.S., our comments will be received if we respond promptly.

I thank you, more than words can express, for this support to care about kids at camp in response to Emily's death and the many ways friends have shown they care.

Very sincerely,

"Emily's mom"

Judy Josey

205

The following is a written response to the public hearing with The Michigan Department of Social Services, Administrative Rules for Children's Camps. I wish to support the need for more attentive regulations to care for the psychological and physical safety rights of children and families during the camp experience.

This is important to me because of the tragic death of Emily Losey this past August while attending soccer camp in Michigan. The following are felt to be important issues after the completion of an investigation of her death.

1. R 400.1004
   ☐ Written policies, procedures, program statements, plans
   Telephone communication shall be made available with permission from the counselor, to make contact with home as needed for emotional support or requests for help. Campers shall not be intimidated upon receiving mail communication.

2. R 400.1005
   ☐ Staff; general requirements
   The inservice training programs for all staff members shall include, in addition to those listed, normal growth and development using a holistic (biophysical, psychosocial, cognitive and spiritual) approach to understand normal expectations, motivation and fears of the children attending the camp.
   The directors of camps shall be able to show educational experience or courses completed in theory and understanding of growth and development.

3. R 400.1011
   ☐ (2) (In addition to the proposed) the health care official shall be licensed by the state for dispensing medication.

   ☐ Physical Examinations
   Athletic camps or camps including extensive physical activity shall require a written physical report by a qualified physician performed within the preceeding 12 months. Physical examination shall include a simple stress test and current B.P. and be presented to the health official upon arrival.

4. R 400.1014
   ☐ The health statement shall inform parents that permission is assumed for treatment for "minor" first aid ailments while at camp and the range of treatment, including prn (as needed) orders, made available as requested to families from the health official upon arrival at camp. Parents shall be invited to contribute to the mandatory physical assessment that is to be conducted within the first 24 hours of their child's camp experience.

   ☐ The written history form shall include in addition to immunizations, allergies and permission for emergency care, a health history with the individualized illness symptoms common to the child, i.e., frequent headaches, fever, kinds of pain experienced, menstrual difficulties and physical reactions to stress.

5. R 400.1015
   ☐ Rule 15. (1)
   (d) Standard health care orders shall include notification of family within 24 hours of onset of ill symptoms or parents given the option of that notification privilege on the written history form.

   (e) First aid and health care supplies to include a blood pressure cuff and stethoscope particularly at athletic camp facilities.

Signed _____

Additional Opinions or Comments _____
_____
_____
_____
_____
_____

ED FREDRICKS
23RD DISTRICT
STATE CAPITOL
LANSING, MICHIGAN 48909
517—373-6920

844 MILLBRIDGE PV
HOLLAND, MICHIGAN 49423
616—392-8418

COMMITTEES ON:
HEALTH & SOCIAL SERVICES
STATE AND VETERANS' AFFAIRS
UPPER PENINSULA INDUSTRIAL
AND ECONOMIC AFFAIRS

Carol Living

February 21, 1984

Ms. Judith M. Losey
1261 Timber Oaks Court
Plainwell, Michigan 49080

Dear Ms. Losey:

Enclosed are some Joint Administrative Rules (#84-14) pertaining to your profession which are now pending in the Joint Committee on Administrative Rules. They will be put on the agenda in the relatively near future and for that reason I am asking that if you desire to have any input on these rules that you respond to my office with your analysis before Friday, March 2.

An explanation of the rules process is as follows: After passage of a law, in most cases, those laws which must be administered by a department require that the department promulgate what are known as Administrative Rules. This is meant to be the fine tuning of the law which is too detailed to actually put in statute. Nevertheless, what often happens is that the department goes far beyond what the legislature intended when it asked for rules.

The legislature must approve these rules before they can go into effect and promulgation is done by the departments submitting these rules to the Joint Committee on Administrative Rules after a somewhat lengthy procedure of hearings and refinements at the department and other administrative levels. The Joint Committee on Administrative Rules consists of Republicans and Democrats from the House and Senate. The rules, in order to go into effect, must pass with the majority of both House and Senate committee members. For this reason, my vote as a member of this committee carries more weight than is the case on other legislative committees. Because I have like-minded support on the committee it is very often possible to completely stymie rules and prevent departments from initiating practices which the legislature did not intend.

-continued-

Scheduled arrival times shall be assigned to campers to
have a health screening interview with the parent, camper
and health official to include the following:

(a)
(b)
(c)   ⟩   as listed in the proposal
(d)

Public Response hearing results.

Letters sent - 1,500
Letters returned - 393 — Total Support - 85%
Responses with remarks: 137
Supporting physical examinations - 88%
Support for parent notification 98%

Incidents of other ill children at camp:

1. Food poisoning - Parents not notified.

2. Girl Scout Camp - became ill in 3rd day - not allowed to
   call home or be excused from activities.
   When taken directly to the Dr - temp 103° and a
   very contagious virus.

3. Girl Scout Camp - daughter age 11, misdiagnosed for aye injury
   Waited 2 days for parents to be notified.
   Child not allowed to call home.

4. Day Camp bus - turned over with the children and all
   taken to the E.R. and parents not notified.

5. Child fell asleep in sun - not found for 2 hrs.
   and spent 3 days in the infirmary. Parents never told
   when the child was picked up nor called at the time.

6. Child broke arm a put into cast from wrist to shoulder
   Parents never aware until picked him up after 2 wks.

7. Girl Scout Camp - UTI - parent not called. Child unconf.
   took 1 mo of tx to heal when if called = 1 day.
   Parent lived 10 min. away.

208

Personal tragedy spurs woman to urge parents to check out children's camps

JACQUELINE MITCHELL
GAZETTE STAFF WRITER

Camping in the great outdoors can be a fun-filled learning experience for most youngsters.

Each year, more than 250,000 young campers in the state attend a variety of camping sites tailored to meet most any child's needs. General camps are offered through the Girl Scouts, Boy Scouts, YMCA, churches and other non-profit organizations, with various camping sessions offered through August.

Special interest camps from marching band and cheerleading to soccer and volleyball are also offered to school-age youngsters.

And camping has proved beneficial to parents. It's a time to get the children out of the house for a week or two and enjoy leisure activities that parents often furego because of the youngsters.

"It's easy to be excited about sending our children to camp for summer fun and learning without thinking about them becoming ill there, and we look forward to the vacation from parenting," said Judith Gruizenga-Ellis, child life clinical specialist at Borgess Medical Center.

But in all of the excitement and anticipation of a camping experience, Gruizenga-Ellis said parents should be "more inquisitive about those who assume total responsibility and health-care decisions for our children."

Gruizenga-Ellis' only child, Emily Losey, died at Camp Wakeshma in Three Rivers in August 1983 at age 11 while playing soccer at the summer camp sponsored by the YMCA of St. Joseph County.

Gruizenga-Ellis, who recently remarried and lives in Plainwell, filed a complaint in April 1984 with the Michigan Department of Social Services Division of Child Day Care Licensing against Camp Wakeshma.

Gruizenga-Ellis said the camp had not notified her that her child was ill until the time of Emily's death.

Gruizenga-Ellis said that "because of Emily's ill symptoms prior to her death, continuation of strenuous play and history of Emily having had a prior episode of a heart block during severe illness, the pathologist believes that the combination was the cause of the death."

According to the autopsy report, Emily's body was "perfectly healthy" with the exception of a small heart anomaly that could develop into difficulties later in life. But, the report

> Parents should be 'more inquisitive about those who assume total responsibility and health-care decisions for our children.'
>
> — Judith Gruizenga-Ellis

said, Emily's heart tissue did not show any unhealthy conditions from the anomaly.

Gruizenga-Ellis said her concern was with "the absence of appropriate assessment of Emily's prior symptoms, inadequate diagnosis and treatment of those symptoms and the neglect of the doctor or family being notified even though her ill symptoms persisted beyond 24-36 hours.

"Those decisions were then made without a physical or adequate history for making appropriate judgments by the health official," Gruizenga-Ellis said.

After a lengthy investigation, the camp licensing division found nothing which "revealed that the camp was at any time not in compliance with the Administrative Rules governing summer camps," according to the investigative report.

Gruizenga-Ellis said she is not completely satisfied with camp regulations and guidelines for child-care programs. As a result, Gruizenga-Ellis compiled a list of areas parents should be aware of before sending there child to camp and while the child is attending the camp.

"Probably the big issue for me is it helps me to care about Emily and kids at camp now that she isn't here any more," Gruizenga-Ellis said. "They are questions I wished I would have asked."

First of all, Gruizenga-Ellis said that parents should check the licensure or accreditations of the camp. Common accreditations are the American Camping Association, Christian Camping International and Michigan State Licensure.

Many accredited camps go beyond basic minimum state requirements, she said. Most states have no requirements but, she added, Michigan recently updated licensure requirements effective for the next ten years.

"Ask about the camp philosophy to see if this particular camp will be compatible with the temperament and interest of your child," Gruizenga-Ellis said.

Parents may want to be alerted to camps which practice harsh disciplinary actions or discourage any kind of interaction with the parents while the child is at the camp, she said.

"Listen for intimidating games and jokes against family contact," Gruizenga-Ellis said. "Support your child's need for family contact and belonging even though the independence-/dependence struggle is active at this age."

She encourages parents to keep communication lines open with their children. Letters and phone calls inquiring about the child's activities, health and adjustments at the camp may help to ease the concern some parents may have or alert them to a potential problem.

Find out who will be in charge of your child by calling the camp director or visit the camp. If you can, to find out who will be supervising your child's group and the environment your child will be living in during the camping sessions, she said.

And, Gruizenga-Ellis said compare the camp's brochure of information with the actual setting to confirm that the camp really delivers the services and programs that are advertised.

"Question whether your child or the children have the freedom to call home if they feel they need to without having to explain or get 'emergency-only' permission," Gruizenga-Ellis said.

"If emergency-only permission exists, ask what qualifies as an emergency," Gruizenga-Ellis said. "Many camps do not allow children to call out at any time for any reason, including illness."

Gruizenga-Ellis said parents should inquire about the camp's emergency plan in case of a serious illness or accident.

"Request to view the 'as needed' physician's guidelines and orders that are already furnished to the camp by a physician who may not know your child," Gruizenga-Ellis said. "It is required by law that they be available by request."

If parents have a complaint about a camp, they may contact the Michigan Department of Social Services Division of Child Welfare Licensing in Lansing.

Printed in the United States
By Bookmasters